Breaking With the Past?
Civil-Military Relations in the
Emerging Democracies of East Asia

About the East-West Center

The East-West Center promotes better relations and understanding among the people and nations of the United States, Asia, and the Pacific through cooperative study, research, and dialogue. Established by the US Congress in 1960, the Center serves as a resource for information and analysis on critical issues of common concern, bringing people together to exchange views, build expertise, and develop policy options.

The Center's 21-acre Honolulu campus, adjacent to the University of Hawai'i at Mānoa, is located midway between Asia and the US mainland and features research, residential, and international conference facilities. The Center's Washington, DC, office focuses on preparing the United States for an era of growing Asia Pacific prominence.

The Center is an independent, public, nonprofit organization with funding from the US government, and additional support provided by private agencies, individuals, foundations, corporations, and governments in the region.

Policy Studies 63

Breaking With the Past?
Civil-Military Relations in the Emerging Democracies of East Asia

Aurel Croissant, David Kuehn,
and Philip Lorenz

Breaking With the Past? Civil-Military Relations in the Emerging Democracies of East Asia
Aurel Croissant, David Kuehn, and Philip Lorenz

ISSN 1547-1349 (print) and 1547-1330 (electronic)
ISBN 978-0-86638-226-7 (print) and 978-0-86638-227-4 (electronic)

Hard copies of all titles, and free electronic copies of most titles, are available from:

East-West Center
1601 East-West Road
Honolulu, Hawai'i 96848-1601
Tel: 808.944.7111
EWCInfo@EastWestCenter.org
EastWestCenter.org/PolicyStudies

In Asia, hard copies of all titles, and electronic copies of select Southeast Asia titles, co-published in Singapore, are available from:

Institute of Southeast Asian Studies
30 Heng Mui Keng Terrace
Pasir Panjang Road, Singapore 119614
publish@iseas.edu.sg
bookshop.iseas.edu.sg

Contents

Executive Summary

Establishing effective civilian control over the military is an important challenge for many newly democratized nations. This is particularly true for East Asia, where militaries wielded considerable political power in the authoritarian past. This study analyses civil-military relations in five new East Asian democracies: Indonesia, the Philippines, South Korea, Taiwan, and Thailand. These countries differ significantly in the pace and trajectory of post-transition civil-military relations and in the extent to which they have been able to establish civilian control. In South Korea and Taiwan, civilians were able to eliminate the military's remaining influence over the political system, while civilian control in Indonesia is yet to be fully institutionalized, civil-military relations in the Philippines are in prolonged crisis, and in Thailand, civilian control and democracy collapsed in the 2006 military coup. Even the successful civilian-led democracies of Northeast Asia struggled before they were able to create effective civilian capacity to oversee and manage defense and military policy.

In order to capture these differences, this study defines civilian control as a distribution of power between elected civilian authorities and military leaders in which civilians can make decisions autonomously and without undue influence from the military in five policy areas: elite recruitment, public policy, internal security, national defense, and military organization.

Based on this conceptualization, this paper first describes the initial conditions from which the transition to democracy began. Although the military was a powerful actor in all of the region's autocracies, the extent to which it was able to dominate differed considerably: Taiwan and the Philippines were led by civilians, South Korea and Thailand were military regimes, while Indonesia was ruled by a civil-military coalition. This had important implications for the development of civil-military relations after the transition: in the formerly military-led and mixed regimes, civilians had to push the remaining military officers from positions of power, while authorities in the formerly civilian-led regimes had to make inroads into domains once reserved for the military, mostly security and defense policy, and prevent military adventurism in times of national crisis.

However, civil-military relations after the transition to democracy cannot be explained by the historical legacies of the authoritarian period alone—strategic action also played an important role. In Korea and Indonesia, prioritization and careful timing enabled civilians to push the military to the sidelines, restructure civil-military relations, and significantly increase civilian control despite decades-long traditions of military intervention in politics. Similarly, in Taiwan, careful maneuvering by civilian presidents allowed them to eliminate the military's remaining political prerogatives and to institutionalize control over defense policy. The behavior of elected civilians in the Philippines and Thailand, however, allowed the military to keep or even reclaim their political power. In the Philippines, civilians courted the military for support in their struggle against political contenders and armed uprisings, while in Thailand, the military toppled the democratic system when it saw its political and institutional interests threatened by the elected prime minister's increasingly personalist rule.

The divergent approaches through which civilians engaged their militaries were influenced by three sets of structural resources and obstacles for strategic action. First, the legacies of the authoritarian regime were conducive to the establishment of civilian control if, as in Taiwan, they provided civilians with existing institutions to monitor and control the military's behavior, or if, as in Indonesia and South Korea, the military's ability to wield autonomous political power was sufficiently reduced during the transition to democracy. In contrast, the absence of meaningful civilian control institutions from the authoritarian period and the military's tradition of collusion with political forces posed serious obstacles to the establishment of civilian control in the Philippines and Thailand.

Second, insurgency movements in Indonesia, Thailand, and the Philippines threatened the state and made the elected government dependent on the military. This reduced both the incentives for and the ability of civilians to eliminate military privileges, especially in the area of internal security. In Korea and Taiwan, the combination of clearly defined external threats and the absence of domestic insurgencies have facilitated civilian control by reducing the military's role as provider of stability and thus allowing a successful cutback of its formerly pronounced internal security role.

Third, the overall process of democratic consolidation affected the institutionalization of civilian control. While civilians in Taiwan and South Korea, and to a lesser extent Indonesia, were supported by a strong societal consensus on the legitimacy and appropriateness of democracy and civilian government, in Thailand and the Philippines civilian political institutions are weak, civilian elites are divided, and the legitimacy of the political order remains contested. Recurring crises of democracy and the incapacity of the political system to accommodate social and political tensions have provided the foundations for the military's continuing involvement in government.

The analysis of civil-military relations in East Asia's emerging democracies suggests three general conclusions. First, open military intervention remains a real danger for recently democratized countries, but civilian control means more than the mere absence of a military coup. As long as the military possesses autonomous decision-making power, the democratically elected authorities' power to govern and the quality of democracy remain limited. Second, strategic action by the civilian authorities is essential for overcoming military resistance to the institutionalization of civilian control. Third, for these strategies to be successful, civilians must pay close attention to the opportunities and resources provided by the structural and historical context in which they find themselves.

The case of Thailand forcefully demonstrates that any attempt to employ robust strategies without the necessary resources not only will fail to reinforce civilian control, but also can lead to the breakdown of both civilian control and democratic rule. There are grounds for optimism about the further consolidation of civilian control and democracy in

Northeast Asian countries and to a lesser extent in Indonesia. However, the deep entrenchment of the military in the Philippines and Thailand, as well as the many political, social, and economic problems these countries face, make significant extension of civilian control unlikely in the medium term.

Breaking With the Past?
Civil-Military Relations in the Emerging Democracies of East Asia

Introduction

In recent decades, several East Asian nations have transitioned from authoritarian rule to democracy. These emerging democracies do not share a single pattern of civil-military relations: Thailand has failed to institutionalize civilian control; civil-military relations in the Philippines are in prolonged crisis; civilian control in Indonesia is yet to be institutionalized; but civilian control has been established in South Korea and Taiwan. Both structural factors and agency (political entrepreneurship) played important roles in the evolution of post-transition civil-military relations.[1]

In Korea and Indonesia, strategic action, prioritization, and careful timing enabled civilians to take advantage of opportunities to restructure civil-military relations and overcome legacies of military intervention in politics. In Thailand, on the other hand, civilians overestimated their ability to influence the military and provoked military intervention. In the Philippines, civilian governments forged a symbiotic relationship with military elites, which allowed civilian governments to survive in office but protected the military's institutional prerogatives.

These differences in the development of civil-military relations also had serious repercussions for national security, political stability, and democratic consolidation. South Korea, Taiwan, and to a lesser degree Indonesia are considered outstanding successes of democratic development and political stability, while Thailand and the Philippines have failed to establish stable democratic systems.

The Nature of Change

Over the past 25 years, East Asia has seen numerous transitions from authoritarian rule to democracy. This has contributed to a general decline of the political power of the armed forces in the region, as is also illustrated by the decreasing frequency of military coups and military regimes (see figure 1).[2] At the same time, however, the quest for civilian control remains high on the political agenda in many new democracies, as democratization has seldom meant the complete depoliticization of the military or full-fledged civilian control. The September 2006 coup in Thailand and five failed coup attempts as well as several mutinies in the Philippines since 1986 indicate that in this part of the world, "the military coup is not a problem of the political past, but a continuing danger, even for electoral democracies that have persisted for over a decade" (Barracca 2007: 138).

Figure 1. Military Regimes and Military Coups in Asia (1950–2011)

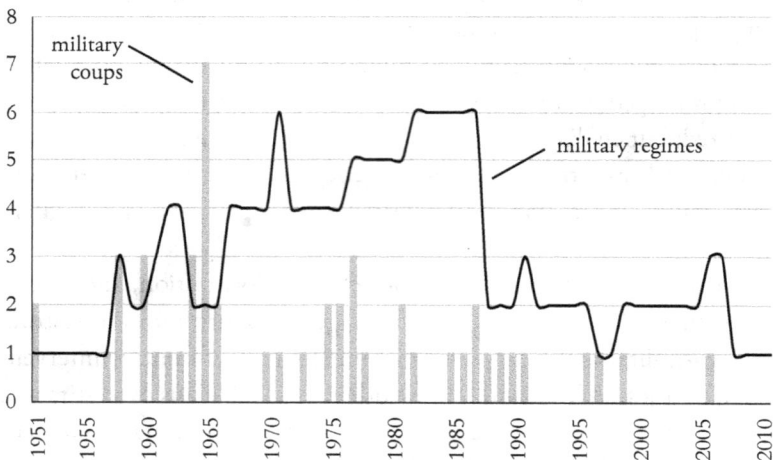

Sources: Powell and Thyne (2011), Hadenius and Teorell (2006), authors' extension.
Note: We have left-truncated the starting years of regimes at 1951 and extended the data for the period 2004–2010.

Civil-military relations in Timor-Leste, while not as unstable as in the Philippines or Thailand, are also strained. In Indonesia, the armed forces (Tentara Nasional Indonesia or TNI) continue to play a significant role in internal security and military organization and enjoy considerable independence from civilian oversight after more than 10 years of democratic reforms. Even South Korea and Taiwan—considered by most observers as success stories of democratic consolidation and the democratic reform of civil-military relations (Diamond 2008)—have struggled to demilitarize government apparatuses and the political decision-making process, dismantle the political management system of the authoritarian order, create robust, credible, and functioning institutions of civilian oversight, and develop strong civilian capacities to manage the security sector.

This ambiguity—the decline of direct forms of military intervention on the one hand and the persistence of military tutelage, prerogatives, and contestation of civilian authority on the other hand—challenges scholars to think more thoroughly about what civilian control is and how it can be achieved. This study aims to address these questions by analyzing developments in civil-military relations in Indonesia, the Philippines, South Korea, Taiwan, and Thailand. These cases are of particular interest because they represent a wide variety of patterns of civil-military relations and differ considerably in their outcomes: Successive civilian governments in the Northeast Asian countries were able to institutionalize civilian control over the armed forces through robust means, and after some difficulties Indonesia also has embarked on a promising trajectory, while the Philippines and Thailand have failed to establish a meaningful degree of civilian control.

The authoritarian regimes from which the transition to democracy began also varied greatly. While South Korea and Thailand were military-led, civilians dominated the regimes in the Philippines and in Taiwan, and Indonesia was ruled by a coalition between a regime party and the military under the leadership of a civilianized president, i.e., a former military officer who retired from active duty. The variation within the region makes it possible to gain important insights into the patterns and processes of civil-military relations in new democracies and to draw robust inferences about the possibilities and limits of institutionalizing civilian control in different historical and political contexts.

The paper proceeds as follows. The following section proposes a multidimensional concept of civilian control that defines it as a distribution of decision-making power between civilian and military leaders. This is followed by an overview of civil-military relations in contemporary East Asia and an analysis of the initial conditions for establishing civilian control in the region. The following two sections analyze civilian control in the five countries that are the focus of this study—first in terms of five key areas in which control is contested, and then in terms of important factors that influence whether or not civilian control will succeed. Finally, the implications of these findings are discussed, both for further research and for the prospects for civilian control in democratizing East Asia.

What Civilian Control Is—and Is Not

Traditionally, civilian control has been defined implicitly as the lack of military coups and military rule or as a low risk for such events (Croissant et al. 2010: 954). The problem with this negative definition is that it ignores more nuanced forms of military influence that are potentially no less harmful for civilian rule—such as the removal of civilian authority over certain policy areas ("reserved domains"; Valenzuela 1992), the ascension of military officers to civilian decision-making positions ("vertical authority"; Pion-Berlin 2003), the isolation of military internal affairs from civilian intrusion, and the dependence of a democratic government on the military to carry out security and development operations inside national borders. To avoid the "fallacy of coup-ism" (Croissant et al. 2010), it is necessary to describe civil-military relations not in terms of dichotomy but as a continuum of decision-making power distributed between civilians and the military.

Civil-military relations should be seen as a continuum of decision-making power distributed between civilians and the military

One proposed definition of civilian control is "that distribution of decision-making power in which civilians have exclusive authority to decide on national politics and their implementation. Under civilian control, civilians can freely choose to delegate decision-making power and the implementation of certain policies to the military while the military has no decision-making power outside those areas specifically defined by civilians. Furthermore, it is civilians alone who determine which particular policies, or aspects of policies, the military implements, and the civilians alone define the boundaries between policy-making and policy-implementation" (Croissant et al. 2010: 955).

Based on this definition, and following insights from Timothy Colton's (1979) analysis of civil-military relations in the Soviet Union and Harold Trinkunas's (2005) work on Latin America, Croissant et al. (2010) conceptualize civilian control as a set of norms, rules, and institutions that structure the balance of decision-making power between civilian institutions and the military in five areas: elite recruitment, public policy, internal security, national defense, and military organization.

- **Elite recruitment** defines the rules, criteria, and processes of recruiting, selecting, and legitimizing political office holders. It reflects the degree to which political processes are open to competition, and the degree of participation, that is, the inclusiveness of political competition (Dahl 1971: 4–6). Civilian control over rules of political competition is undermined when public offices are excluded from open competition and when the military influences electoral procedures. It is also constrained if the military enjoys constitutionally reserved representation in cabinet and parliament, has formal or informal veto power over the appointment of officials, or controls the electoral process, or if active-duty personnel hold positions of political leadership.

  When an active-duty officer serves on a national security council, or is appointed as defense minister, this constrains civilian authority but does not call into question the civilian nature of the government—so long as military influence is contained within the defense sphere, the elected president is commander-in-chief, and civilians retain a majority on the security council and continue to make the nation's policies. The civilian nature of the government is, however, called into question when the military acquires nondefense cabinet portfolios and legislative presentation in large numbers (Pion-Berlin 2003: 12).

- **Public policy** comprises the rules and processes of policymaking (agenda setting, policy formulation, and policy adoption) and policy implementation. Military influence over these procedures provides the military an opportunity to influence, veto, or even determine social, economic, and political policies. Consequently, the degree of civilian control depends on the extent of military influence over the policymaking process and over state agencies charged with implementing policy.

- **Internal security** entails all decisions and measures regarding possible deployments of the military to keep peace, order, and security within national boundaries (for example, in riot control, domestic law enforcement, border control, counterterrorism, and to put down insurrections), as well as the military's provision of logistical support and restoration of civilian infrastructure during its involvement in development operations (see Rasmussen 1999; Collier 1999; Trinkunas 2005; Wilkinson 2006). Measures of the degree of civilian control in this area are the extent to which civilians have the authority to establish the military's mission and goals and the principles and guidelines that govern its operations, and the extent of the military's ability to dominate nonmilitary security forces, law enforcement agencies, and the national intelligence apparatus.

- **National defense**—that is, safeguarding the nation's territory against external military threats—is traditionally the primary role of any armed force. Even though most military forces in the post–Cold War era reoriented from territorial defense to new missions such as humanitarian aid, disaster relief, and multilateral peacekeeping, this shift did not formally supplant territorial defense as their primary function. Especially in nations that face high levels of external threats, there is broad cooperation between military and civilian elites, and military officers are involved in the formulation of defense policy.

  Effective and efficient defense policies require that civilians use the military's professional expertise. Therefore, it is not surprising that the military plays an important role in national defense (Pion-Berlin 2005; Pion-Berlin and Trinkunas 2007; Bruneau and Trinkunas 2006). Nonetheless, for civilian control over this area to exist, civilians must ultimately make the policy decisions.

- **Military organization** comprises policies that define the mission, roles, and structure of the military—decisions about acquisitions, logistics, training, and equipment, as well as personnel management and military promotions. While the military needs a certain degree of autonomy in order to fulfill its mission, civilian control requires that civilians be able to define its range and boundaries. The ultimate indicator of civilian control in this arena is the extent to which civilians can define and enforce the limits of military regulation of its internal affairs, and who has the ultimate say when it comes to conflict between civilians and officers.

For Latin America, Pion-Berlin (1997) has demonstrated that impediments to full civilian control are especially strong in this area. One reason for this is that attempts to expand civilian authority over the military's internal affairs are often perceived by military leaders as an assault on the professional integrity, cohesion, and identity of the military. Another important reason is the lack of strong civilian capabilities and institutions for managing military affairs.

Full-fledged civilian control, at least in principle, requires that civilian authorities enjoy uncontested decision-making power in all five areas—while in the ideal-type military regime, military officers dominate all decisions concerning political structures, processes, and policies and civilians possess no autonomous political authority except in those areas specifically defined by the military. The reality in many emerging democracies, however, is more ambiguous, as the extent of civilian and military influence varies in different areas and over time. Often, civil-military relations are characterized by overlapping or shared competencies, areas of contestation, delegation of responsibilities, and informal networking between military officers and civilian elites. Consequently, only by disaggregating civil-military relations into the five decision-making areas, in these cases of shared responsibility (Bland 1999), can their positions along the continuum of civil-military distribution of power be systematically evaluated (Croissant et al. 2010: 955).

In addition to defining civilian control, it is important to note what civilian control is not. First, it is not the same as democratic control. While "democracy isn't possible without civilian control of the military," the experiences of civil-military relations in communist one-party regimes illustrate that "civilian control of the military is clearly possible without democracy" (Forster 2006: 96). In any authoritarian regime, the military is a crucial partner (Ezrow and Frantz 2011), but government office holders need to keep the military's political aspirations in check. This is true not only for civilian-led regimes, such as the absolute monarchies of the Middle East or one-party states in different parts of the world (cf. Henry and Springborg 2001; Perlmutter and LeoGrande 1982; Joo 1995; Betz 2004), but also for military regimes in which the "military-as-government" needs to maintain the loyalty of the "military-as-institution" (Alagappa 2001a: 8).

Second, civilian control is not the only issue in civil-military relations (Feaver 1999). Other examples include the degree to which the military is able to achieve the goals assigned to it by political leaders (effectiveness) and the cost in lives and resources necessary to do so (efficiency) (Bruneau 2005: 2012). Nonetheless, most scholars consider the question of "who guards the guardians" the most important issue in the study of civil-military relations (Feaver 1996; Pion-Berlin 2011).

Third, effective civilian control implies neither effectiveness and efficiency in civil-military relations (Bruneau and Goetze 2006: 71) nor good governance in the security sector. It simply ensures that civilians are responsible for political decision making (Trinkunas 2005: 8). Even in the democratic new member states of the European Union and NATO in Eastern and Central Europe, the practices of civilian control often do not fit the normative ideal of democratic security sector governance (Forster 2006), which includes not only effective control of the military by democratically elected civilian authorities but also, among other things, parliamentary oversight, transparent decision making, civil society participation, ensuring that military training is in line with democratic norms and values, and providing human security (cf. Hänggi 2004).

Fourth, the idea of civilian control assigns the military the role of defending society, not defining it (Kohn 1997: 142). But it does not assume an apolitical military. Israel, for example, is a liberal democracy with a great degree of interconnection between military and civilian elites, and a close involvement of military leaders in government policy formation

> *Under civilian control, the military defends society, it does not define it. But this does not assume an apolitical military*

within the normative framework of generally accepted civilian control (Kamvara 2000: 75). The question for civilian control is therefore not whether the military yields political influence, but how and how much.

Civil-Military Relations in Contemporary East Asia

The countries of East Asia are particularly useful cases for analyzing civil-military relations in new democracies. East Asia today shows a remarkable variation of regime types. Based on the Bertelsmann Transformation Index (Bertelsmann Stiftung 2012), the political regimes in the region can be broadly classified into three categories: liberal, defective, and failed democracies (see Merkel 2004, table 1).[3]

Table 1. Regime Types in Northeast and Southeast Asia

		Northeast Asia	Southeast Asia
"Second wave" democracy		Japan	
"Third wave" democracies	Liberal	South Korea, Taiwan	
	Flawed		Indonesia, Philippines, Timor-Leste
	Failed		Cambodia, Thailand
Autocracies		China North Korea	Brunei, Burma, Laos, Malaysia, Singapore, Vietnam

Sources: Croissant and Bünte 2011; Bertelsmann Stiftung 2012.

The first category comprises the well-established democracy of Japan, which institutionalized democracy during the "second wave of democratization" (Huntington 1991) in 1947[4]. The second category includes seven countries that experienced a political transition to democracy during Huntington's "third wave" (in the last two decades or so). In Northeast Asia, these are South Korea (1988) and Taiwan (1992), and in Southeast Asia, Cambodia (1992), Timor-Leste (2002), Indonesia (1998), the Philippines (1986), and Thailand (1992).

Depending on the degree to which these countries have been successful in consolidating democracy and guaranteeing a substantial array of political and civil rights, they can be further differentiated into liberal, flawed, and failed democracies. In the first two subcategories, elections have become the accepted method of transferring political power and choosing legislative representatives and the chief executive. These groups differ, however, in the quality of democracy, the stability of the political process, and the extent to which democracy has achieved legitimacy and popular support among both the broader populace and the political elites. While the Northeast Asian cases combine a functional democratic regime of free and fair elections with robust protection of civil liberties and political rights and a strong degree of horizontal accountability and rule of law, the Southeast Asian "third wave" democracies suffer from a variety of institutional flaws (Merkel 2004). The third subcategory comprises two countries in which new authoritarian regimes have been established after democratic transformation failed: Cambodia and Thailand.

The third category, autocracies, includes a large and heterogeneous group of regimes that have never made the transition to democracy. They range from the soft "electoral authoritarian regimes" (Schedler 2006) in Singapore and Malaysia to one-party "closed autocracies" (Diamond 2002) in Laos, Vietnam, North Korea, and the People's Republic of China, to the military-dominated regime in Burma. In "electoral authoritarian regimes," formal democratic institutions coexist with authoritarian political practices, and elections are the principal means for acquiring political power (Levitsky and Way 2010; Case 2011). "Closed autocracies" strictly limit political competition to segments within the ruling coalition.

The new democracies in the region differ not only in the degree of successful democratic consolidation but also in the nature of the authoritarian regimes from which they developed. Although the military is a crucial partner in any authoritarian regime (Ezrow and Frantz 2011), there are significant differences in the bargaining power of dictators, party elites, and military leaders—both between types of authoritarian regimes and within any given dictatorship over time (ibid.; Svolik 2009).

Some democracies, such as Taiwan, the Philippines, and Cambodia, developed from civilian-led authoritarian regimes, and others (South Korea and Thailand) from regimes "in which military officers [were] major or predominant political actors by virtue of their actual or threatened use of force" (Nordlinger 1977: 2), while Indonesia moved from a civilianized military–multiparty coalition regime (Mietzner 2011) to democratic rule (see table 2). Many authors have highlighted the importance of initial conditions, resulting from the character of the previous regime, for the development of an emerging democracy.

Given the variance summarized in table 3, East Asia is particularly promising as a source of insights into civil-military relations in new democracies and their effects on democratic quality and consolidation. Five cases are particularly interesting: South Korea and Taiwan present similarly successful cases of institutionalizing civilian control and liberal democracy despite their significant differences in initial conditions. Indonesia and the Philippines cover the middle ground, in terms of both democratization and civilian control. And in Thailand, democracy has failed due to a military coup against a democratically elected prime minister.

Table 2. Authoritarian Regimes that Preceded East Asian "Third Wave" Democracies

Type of transition to democracy	Type of authoritarian regime	
	Civilian-dominated	Military-dominated
Result of international intervention	Cambodia	Timor-Leste*
Negotiated by regime and opposition		Indonesia,* South Korea, Thailand
Initiated by regime	Taiwan	
Led by the opposition	Philippines	

Source: Croissant and Kuehn 2011a. Categories of transition to democracy are based on Huntington (1991: 113–115) and Shin and Tusalem (2009: 361).
* From 1975 to 1999, Timor-Leste was occupied by Indonesia. The Indonesian New Order under General Suharto began as a military regime, but in the 1980s became more civilianized and less dominated by the military. The new democracies of Northeast and Southeast Asia also differ significantly in the extent to which they have been able to institutionalize civilian control.

Table 3. Civilian Control in East Asian "Third Wave" Democracies (2011)

	Regime type		
	Liberal democracy	Flawed democracy	Failed democracy
Civilian control	South Korea, Taiwan		
Conditional military subordination		Indonesia, Philippines, Timor-Leste	Cambodia
Military control			Thailand

Source: Croissant and Kuehn 2011a; see also Siaroff 2009: 92.

Timor-Leste and Cambodia, while important and fascinating in their own right, are less significant for a comparative analysis of civil-military relations in new democracies. Unlike in most "third wave" democracies, developments in these countries were heavily influenced by external actors, the respective United Nations transitional authorities.

Initial Conditions that Influence Civil-Military Relations

Scholars have frequently noted the influence of different initial conditions, authoritarian legacies, and paths to democracy on the development of civil-military relations in post-authoritarian countries. For example, Zoltan Barany (1997) identifies the lack of substantive traditions of military interventionism and the communist officer corps's strong belief in the principle of civilian control as key factors for the relatively smooth transition from communist to democratic civilian control in most post-communist countries in Eastern Europe and the former Soviet Union. In contrast, Latin Americanists have traced many problems of civilian control over the military in the region to the legacies of military rule and the evolution of civil-military relations in the 20th century (Loveman 1999).

For Asian countries, researchers also stress the importance of historical factors during the formation of state, nation, and polity as key variables for the evolution of contemporary civil-military relations. For example, Muthiah Alagappa argues that, due to their role in the processes of decolonization and nation- and state-building, Asian militaries often demanded a privileged status as guardian of the nation (Alagappa 2001a: 9). As a consequence, their mission profiles diversified and expanded over time: Eventually, military personnel became heavily engaged in political decision making, commercial activities, social development, and civic action projects, and in putting down internal insurrections.

Finally, Felipe Agüero, in comparative research on Latin America and southern Europe, emphasizes the different roles the armed forces play in transfers of power as key explanations for the differences both between and within the regions (Agüero 1998: 384; 2001: 207–209). While he argues that the nature of the authoritarian regime matters, as challenges in civil-military reforms are especially acute and arduous in transitions from military rule to democracy, he emphasizes the extent of military control over the process of transition: the stronger the military influence, the more of its prerogatives will survive the transition and the more it will be able to stifle post-authoritarian reforms (Agüero 1995: 139–153).

In East Asia, there are some important similarities regarding the nature of civil-military relations in the authoritarian period (Croissant and Kuehn 2009: 191). In the five East Asian countries that have made the transition to democracy since the 1980s, the military had been a powerful political actor and integral shareholder in the authoritarian elite coalition. The armed forces had pervasive influence on political issues beyond pure defense matters, and performed various roles including national security, police work, development activities, and nation building. Authoritarian rulers have time and again relied on military coercion to guarantee regime security and maintain law and order. Furthermore, according to military folklore in Indonesia and Thailand, the armed forces created the nation. Even in South Korea, Taiwan, and the Philippines, where the military's role as an agent of nation building had been less accentuated, the armed forces imagined themselves as the warrantors of national survival and defenders against communist subversion.

Such common characteristics notwithstanding, a careful analysis reveals fundamental differences in the relations between the authoritarian regimes and their armed forces, and their roles in the transitions—which, in turn, had a profound impact on civil-military relations in post-authoritarian politics. Among the regions touched by the "third wave," East Asia stands out because of the heterogeneous nature of the authoritarian regimes and their civil-military relations. In Latin America, authoritarian regimes were essentially controlled by military elites, while in communist Eastern Europe, civilians controlled the government. In East Asia, however, the variety of authoritarian regimes included civilian authoritarianism in Taiwan and the Philippines, military authoritarianism in Thailand and South Korea,

> *East Asia experienced a variety of authoritarian regimes, as well as considerable variation within individual countries*

and civilianized military rule in Indonesia. Moreover, there was considerable variation within individual countries: the political power of military officers changed over time, as did the degree to which the military's power was institutionalized and the extent of separation between the military-as-institution and the military-as-government.

Indonesia

Particularly in Indonesia, the ability of the armed forces to influence government policies changed significantly. The Indonesian military had played an important role in the struggle against Dutch colonialism, a fact bolstered by its own historiography (McGregor 2007). Following almost two decades of civilian rule, first under parliamentary democracy and then under President Sukarno's Guided Democracy, the self-proclaimed New Order regime originated in a slow-motion military takeover by Major General Suharto from 1965 to 1967 (Crouch 1979). After coming to power, the original junta government became increasingly personalized as Suharto successfully marginalized his military comrades.

Nonetheless, until the late 1970s the military remained the predominant political force within the regime, second only to the president (Slater 2010: 133). It exercised full control over the security apparatus and defense policies and defined its primary roles as defender of the nation against internal enemies and primary agent of sociopolitical development. This was reflected in the institutional overlap of military and civilian administrative functions under the territorial command system. Based on the creation of a socio-political role for the military under the dual-function (*dwifungsi*) doctrine and the practice of promoting active-duty military personnel to nonmilitary duties (*kekaryaan*), the military had privileged access to the political center, policymaking, and public administration at every level of the state bureaucracy (Honna 2003). Therefore, military officers were able to exert considerable influence on public policy and elite recruitment.

In the late 1970s, the military's position as the most powerful institution deteriorated as Suharto's rule grew increasingly personalistic. Suharto's use of the military promotion system, patronage politics, and divide-and-conquer strategies to control the military had started to generate internal divisions: he circumscribed the military's political influence by playing off military factions in parliament and Golkar, the regime party that had been created as a joint vehicle for military and bureaucratic political domination, against each other.

When the president began civilizing Golkar during the late 1980s, the military was no longer able to influence politics without Suharto's backing (Tomsa 2008: 39). Existing institutions of civil-military relations were turned into a "franchise" system (McLeod 2008: 200): officers looking for career opportunities had to find individual access to political and economic resources in order to pay their superior officers for promotions. Individual rent-seeking became paramount to military institutional interest and influence. Territorial units had to earn most of their budget through business activities (Mietzner 2009: 48; Mahroza 2009: 51), and individual officers and rank-and-file military personnel quickly became involved in illicit activities like racketeering, smuggling, or gambling (Hadiz 2010: 74).

The importance of fund-raising and good connections to the ruling clique factionalized the military leadership and turned Suharto into the ultimate arbiter of internal conflict. Consequently, "what started as a system of oligarchic military rule evolved into a highly personalized regime, backed in nearly equal measure by military and civilian organizations" (Slater 2010: 133). Meanwhile, Suharto could rely on the army to control and, if necessary, repress political parties, trade unions, student movements, religious leaders, and newspapers (Aspinall 2005).

Indonesia entered the transition to democracy (*reformasi*) in the wake of the Asian financial crisis in 1998, which drained state coffers, hampered Suharto's ability to maintain his patronage network, and forced him to step down. The military leadership had opposed the use of military force against protesters, while the remaining Suharto loyalists among the top brass were in no position to block the transition (T. Lee 2009). When Suharto's vice-president Habibie took office as interim head of government to usher in democratic reforms, one of the main demands by pro-democracy groups and the public was military withdrawal from politics.

Philippines

Unlike in Indonesia, the military's role as an agent of nation-building in the Philippines had been less accentuated. Historically, the Armed Forces of the Philippines (AFP) had been controlled by Congress, the president, and local oligarchs who exploited their influence over military appointments as a bargaining chip for political competition (Anderson 1998: 213; Hedman 2001: 168).

Notwithstanding the more-or-less-working system of civilian control, the AFP also considered itself a vanguard of the modern state and a bulwark against communist subversion (McCoy 2000). Given the 1952 Mutual Defense Treaty, in which the United States guaranteed the country's external security, the AFP concentrated on internal security and was structured, equipped, and trained for counterinsurgency operations (Hall 2010: 29–30; Arugay 2010: 9). Immediately after independence in 1946, the Communist Party of the Philippines and its military arm rebelled against the government. As a result, the military was already engaged in various political and social activities by the early 1950s, and gained decision-making power in these areas. The military was deputized to help guarantee orderly elections, and under President Magsaysay (1953–1957), military civic action projects mushroomed with numerous active-duty military officers appointed to civil posts in government (Berlin 2008: 42–78).

While the military lost much power in the following years, under President Ferdinand Marcos (1965–1986), it recovered political influence (Ciron 1993). With the support of senior police and military officers, the democratically elected president declared martial law in 1972, effectively destroying the democratic system. Marcos appointed officers to key posts in the civilian administration and public enterprises, increased the military budget by more than 700 percent between 1972 and 1985, and increased the size of the military from 62,000 in 1972 to 159,000 in 1986 (Ciron 1993, table 5.5).

At the same time, the president took control of military promotions and used this to forge a strong alliance with the military by filling military leadership positions with his relatives, friends from his native region, and former classmates from the University of the Philippines cadet corps. In the early 1980s, "the AFP looked more like Marcos's Praetorian Guard than a properly professional military" (Hedman 2001: 178). Marcos' strategy of consolidating his personal control over the military had far-reaching implications, as it created factional competition within the armed forces (I. Kim 2008: 41).

The frustration of junior and middle-ranking officers with the widespread corruption in the military, the lack of professionalism, promotions based on favoritism, and the government's inability to develop an effective approach to the threats of communist rebellion and Muslim secessionism led to the formation of the Reform Armed Forces

Movement in 1985 (Ciron 1993). On February 22, 1986, 300 Reform Armed Forces Movement officers led by Defense Minister Enrile and the vice chief of staff of the AFP, General Fidel Ramos, staged a coup d'état. The coup failed but facilitated the People's Power mass mobilization against the dictator. Within a few days, almost 90 percent of all army units had declared their support for the military rebels and the civilian opposition (T. Lee 2009: 649).

Marcos's exile in February 1986 set the stage for contestation between a deeply politicized and factionalized

> *Since Marcos's regime was built on informal networks and personal connections, there were no working institutions of civilian oversight or control*

military on one hand and disunified civilians on the other (Thompson 1995). Since Marcos's regime was built on informal networks and personal connections, there were no working institutions of civilian oversight or control. The collapse of military hierarchy, the lack of effective institutions, the sudden breakdown of the authoritarian regime, and the contested legitimacy of the new democratic government created an ideal environment for rogue factions within the AFP to seek control of the political center. Thus, in the early years after the transition, democracy was under constant pressure from the military.

Thailand

In Thailand, the military had dominated politics and the state for most of the 20th century (Yawnghwe 1997). From the coup of 1932, which ended absolute monarchy, into the 1970s, military intervention seemed to be the accepted mode of transition between governments. From 1939 until 1973 (with a brief interregnum from 1944 to 1947), a series of military dictators ruled the country. Thai politics was characterized by a "vicious cycle of military coups" (Chai-anan 1982: 1995) in which one military faction staged a coup against the military regime in power and attempted to legitimize and institutionalize its political ambitions by passing a new constitution before being overthrown by a competing military clique. Between 1932 and September 2006, Thailand saw

18 coups and the same number of constitutions, eight of which were abolished by military coup (Traimas and Hoerth 2008: 302).

The military's prominence in Thai politics was founded not only on its self-image as ultimate guardian of state, nation, and monarchy, but also on its wide-ranging nontraditional functions in national development and internal security provision; these legitimized its political activism and provided opportunities for the military leadership to engage in lucrative economic activities (Ockey 2001; Chambers 2010b; Croissant and Kuehn 2011b: 214). At the same time, the military's role expansion fueled factionalism between the military services and among military academy graduating classes, which competed for political influence and access to rents (Wyatt 1984; Surachart 1999).

Long-term processes of economic and social change, together with the rise of private business and party politics in the 1970s, weakened the power of the generals and bureaucrats. In the early 1980s, this led to a gradual liberalization and the emergence of a soft authoritarian regime overseen by the king. Army Commander Gen. Prem Tinsulanond was appointed prime minister. He was not accountable to the elected House of Representatives (lower house), which had to share political power with an appointed Senate (upper house), whose members came primarily from the state bureaucracy and the armed forces (Lihkit 1992; Chai-anan 1995). However, political liberalization initiated under Prem's government (1980–1988) culminated in a short-lived democratic interregnum with an elected prime minister (1988–1991).

Growing military suspicion of civilian interference in its domain led to a coup in February 1991, a new constitution in December 1991, and parliamentary elections in 1992, after which armed forces commander Gen. Suchinda Kraprayoon was named prime minister. The new regime, however, suffered from a serious lack of legitimacy, and mass protests commenced in May 1992, aimed at forcing the military from power. After the military violently cracked down on the protesters, killing numerous unarmed civilians, the king intervened to ease Suchinda out of office and initiated a political transition. After the September 1992 parliamentary elections, a coalition cabinet under the civilian Prime Minister Chuan Leekpai took office. Still, the military was able to defend its political and institutional autonomy, along with significant political prerogatives, such as representation of active-duty officers in the Senate (Surarchart 1999).

South Korea

In South Korea, the military acted decisively to shape national politics from 1961 to 1988, intervening twice to oust the government. In 1961, a group of reformists from the Korean Military Academy, led by Major General Park Chung-hee, staged a coup (Han 1974). Afterward, Park quickly marginalized the ruling junta. He retired from the military, after the passage of a new constitution in 1963, to rule the country as a quasi-civilian president with the strong backing of the military.

Park's regime, while increasingly repressive, transformed the poverty-stricken country into one of the fastest-growing economies in the world. Under Park's ideology of Total Security, Korean society was systematically organized into a kind of garrison state (Y.M. Kim 2004: 123). Measured in relation to the GNP and government spending, military expenditure was one of the highest in the world (Croissant 2004). In the early 1980s, almost 16 percent of the male population was part of the armed forces, either on active duty or as part of the reserve force (Croissant 2004). At the same time, Park recruited ex-generals into his government and placed a large number of officers in strategic posts in the civilian administration, state enterprises, and foreign service (Moon and Rhyu 2011), making the armed forces the most important channel for upward mobility in Korean society.

After Park's assassination in 1979, Major General Chun Doohwan, then commander of the Defense Security Command, staged a mutiny within the military in December 1979 and then seized political power in May 1980. Known as the Hanahoe (Group One), his faction had occupied key positions in the security apparatus in the final years of Park's dictatorship.[5] In contrast to his predecessor, Chun did not establish personal control, but relied on the collective leadership of the Hanahoe faction (Y.M. Kim 2004: 126). Its active members occupied strategically important posts in key military units and military intelligence agencies, while retired members took over essential posts in the presidential secretariat, the ruling Democratic Justice Party, and the intelligence service (cf. Moon and Rhyu 2011).

As in 1963, the military adopted a new constitution and promised indirect presidential elections after the end of President Chun's single seven-year term in 1987, in order to guarantee political stability. However, when Chun designated Roh Tae-woo, one of the Hanahoe coup leaders of 1980, as his successor, major demonstrations erupted throughout the country.

The government was deterred from imposing martial law by opposition from the United States as well as from non-Hanahoe officers within the military (I. Kim 2008: 50; Ooi 2010). Consequently, Roh Tae-woo declared a plan for political reform on June 29, 1987, paving the way for democratization, the adoption of a new constitution, and direct presidential elections in 1988, which Roh won against a split opposition (M. Lee 1990). The rapid change after decades of military rule was possible because, unlike military regimes in Latin America and Southeast Asia, Korea's military could not place extensive and lasting constraints on the democratic successor regime. Not only was military rule "quasi-civilianized" (Finer 1962) "rather than direct and institutional" (Y.M. Kim 2004: 121), but the military never had access to institutional, financial, or technological resources independent of the government. Most importantly, the military was internally divided between the dominant Hanahoe faction and the large majority of marginalized officers who felt excluded from military leadership positions, so that during the 1987 mass demonstrations most military officers had little incentive to defend the military government against its opponents (I. Kim 2008: 14).

Taiwan

Finally, in Taiwan, the relationship between state and armed forces originally resembled the party-military relations in many communist countries. Founded in 1924 as the military wing of the Nationalist Party or Kuomintang, the National Army played a crucial role in enforcing the political agenda of party leader Generalissimo Chiang Kai-shek on the mainland. Following the Kuomintang's defeat by the communists and its retreat to Taiwan in 1949, the military was modernized and became the main instrument for enforcing party rule over the local Taiwanese population.

During the martial law period, from 1949 to 1987, the military was charged with defending the Kuomintang's hold on power against communist invasion and played a major role in providing internal regime security (Kuehn 2008). This was reflected in a strong representation of military officers in civilian institutions of party and state—such as the party's major decision-making bodies, the public services, and state-owned enterprises—and, especially, the prevalence of military officers in the National Security Council and the military's command over the Taiwan Garrison Command. The Taiwan Garrison Command was responsible for monitoring and combating the political opposition, border control, censorship, domestic intelligence gathering, overseeing the local administration and judiciary, and coordinating civilian police services (Tien 1989: 111).

Though institutional mechanisms for party control were in place, such as the political commissar system and the Political Warfare System (Shih 1990; Bullard 1997), the army enjoyed broad autonomy in matters of national defense and internal security, as defense-related agencies such as the Ministry of National Defense, the National Security Council, and the Kuomintang's Military Affairs Committee were packed with active-duty military officers (Kuehn 2008).

From the late 1960s on, however, the military's political power slowly declined. Although military and party institutions remained closely connected and the military retained its prerogatives in the areas of internal security, defense, and internal affairs, the following decades saw the steady rise of civilian technocrats within the party. As a result of successful economic policies, the need for coercion to maintain political stability decreased, and the importance of the military as an instrument for regime security was reduced. At the same time, the Taiwanization of party and state after the transition of power from Chiang Kai-shek to his son Ching-kuo eased the internal cleavages between the Taiwanese islanders, who felt excluded from regular promotion, and the minority of Chinese mainlander officers, who had long monopolized military leadership positions. Therefore, when Chiang Ching-kuo and his successor, native Taiwanese Lee Teng-hui, initiated the

> *Throughout Taiwan's gradual and carefully prepared transition, the military remained neutral and played no active role*

transition to democracy in the late 1980s, military subordination to the president and the party elite was robustly established. Throughout the gradual and carefully prepared transition, the military remained neutral and played no active role (Kuehn 2008).

Table 4 summarizes the differences and similarities in civil-military relations under authoritarian rule in the five East Asian countries. The differences in military dominance (strong in South Korea and Thailand, weaker in Indonesia, and least in Taiwan and the Philippines), and the contrasts in the behavior of the armed forces during the transfer of power (least active in Taiwan, decisive in the Philippines), translated into different initial conditions and institutional legacies, which strongly affected civil-military relations in the post-transitional era. These factors influenced the leverage of civilian authorities over the military and limited the possible interaction strategies for civilians and the military leadership. However, as the following analysis will demonstrate, such factors do not determine the outcomes of reforms in civil-military relations after democratization. Contrary to what many observers had predicted, democratization resulted in an increase of civilian control in South Korea and Indonesia, while Thailand and the Philippines did not achieve the kind of progress that seemed possible in the mid and late 1990s.

Table 4. Initial Conditions Influencing Civil-Military Relations

	Indonesia	Philippines	South Korea	Taiwan	Thailand
Origin of authoritarian regime	Military coup by senior officers	Civilian autogolpe	Factional military coup	Revolutionary	Military coup by senior officers
Type of authoritarian regime	Civilianized military regime	Civilianized	Non-hierarchical military regime	Civilianized	Hierarchical military regime
Transition substantially affected by the military?	Yes	Yes	Yes	No	Yes
Substantial divisions within the military?	Yes	Yes	Yes	No	Yes
Tradition of civilian control?	No	Yes	No	Yes	No
Expansion of military role	High	High	High	High	High

Civilian Control in Five Key Decision-Making Areas

In order to assess the degree of civilian control over the armed forces in the five East Asian democracies, this section explores the five key decision-making areas discussed earlier: elite recruitment, public policy, internal security, national defense, and military organization. For the sake of brevity, analysis is limited to the most relevant differences and similarities between the cases, focusing especially on states that occupy the extreme ends of the spectrum.[6]

Elite Recruitment and Public Policy

In Taiwan, civilian dominance over these core areas had already been established when democratization started in 1987. In spite of a strong representation of senior military officers in all major government and party structures, the armed forces had not constituted an alternative channel for political ascension, nor was the military able to control political decision making. During the early years of democratization, however, it seemed as if the armed forces' political influence was increasing.

Confronted with opposition from the conservative mainlander faction in the Kuomintang Central Committee, President Lee Teng-hui (1988–2000) decided to appease and co-opt the military, naming former army general and long-term Chief of General Staff Hau Pei-tsun prime minister in 1990. Making Hau head of government did not lead to a significant or lasting increase in military influence, though. First of all, Lee was able to do away with many of the military's institutional means of influencing policy, for instance by transforming the National Security Council, a formerly military-dominated quasi-governmental agency that had the power to veto the budget bill, into a mere presidential advisory body (Lo 2001: 152–56; Swaine 1999: 15).

Furthermore, Hau Pei-tsun retired in 1993, which marked the end of the last remnants of direct military influence on elite recruitment and public policymaking (Fravel 2002: 63–67). Both President Lee and his successor, Chen Shui-bian (2000–2008), strengthened the government's position vis-à-vis the military by promoting professional military personnel and increasing the share of native Taiwanese in the military leadership. This proved an important asset in counterbalancing conservative elements in the officer corps and gradually reduced the military's potential to oppose changes in public policy (Shambaugh 1996: 1292; W. Lee 2007: 210–21).

Even in regard to foreign policy and the highly sensitive topic of relations with mainland China, there is no empirical evidence to suggest undue political involvement of the military or civil-military conflicts. The litmus test for civilian control came in 2000, when Chen Shui-bian, a stout proponent of Taiwan independence and a critic of the military, was elected president. Then-Chief of General Staff Tang Yao-ming publicly pledged loyalty to the new president, emphasizing that the military respected the core principles of democracy (Hsueh 2003). When Chen became president, the military had already shed its influence over public policy, and its departure from political institutions was complete.

In South Korea, the transitional government of President Roh Tae-woo (1988–1993), himself a former coup plotter, refrained from seriously reforming civil-military relations (Kim, Liddle, and Said 2006: 252–54). After inauguration, Roh consolidated his authority over the military by reshuffling key positions (Y.M. Kim 2004: 128), while Hanahoe members continued to receive preferential treatment in promotion. While Roh had the military intelligence apparatus reorganized, the size of the Defense Security Command reduced, and its agents withdrawn from the National Assembly (Graham 1991: 128), implementation of these reforms remained incomplete (Saxer 2004: 389). While this approach helped to shield the fragile government from possible military adventurism, it did nothing to strengthen civilian control.

In contrast to his predecessor, President Kim Young-sam (1993–1998) paid close attention to civil-military relations from the very beginning of his presidential term. Kim had won the presidential election of December 1992 as a candidate of Roh Tae-woo's Democratic Liberal Party, but dissociated himself from his predecessor by choosing the official title of "civilian and democratic government" for his administration (W. Kim 2008: 158). The transition from Roh to Kim was accompanied by a large-scale reshuffle of military posts. Relying on a network of loyal military supporters who came mainly from the president's native Pusan and South Kyongsang region, Kim neutralized military opposition and strengthened his own position (Jun 2001: 131).

In addition, Kim's administration purged senior Hanahoe members from the officer corps and transferred all mid-ranking officers belonging to the faction to units along the border with North Korea, "far away from their previous posts near Seoul" (I. Kim 2008: 74). The once powerful faction was ultimately marginalized when Chun Doo-hwan and Roh Tae-woo, together with 13 other generals, were put on trial in 1996 (Kim, Liddle, and Said 2006: 151). Military representation in the cabinet, National Assembly, and state enterprises was also significantly reduced (see table 5).

Table 5. Retired Military Officers in the Cabinet, National Assembly, and State Enterprises in South Korea (1948–2002)

Regime	Cabinet members (%)	Executives of state enterprises (%)	National Assembly Delegates (%)
Rhee Syngman (1948–1960)	8.2	—*	1.5
Chang Myon (1960–1961)	4.4	—	3.6
Military government (1961–1963)	47.1	—	—
Park Chung-hee (1963–1979)	25.6	—	18.2
Chun Doh-hwan (1980–1988)	19.4	48.5	9.0
Roh Tae-woo (1988–1993)	17.2	38.0	6.8
Kim Young-sam (1993–1998)	5.0	12.4	7.0
Kim Dae-jung (1998–2002)	6.7	6.2	2.2

Source: Croissant 2004; Moon and Rhyu 2011.
* No data were available for these years.

However, even after the neutralization of Hanahoe and the significant reduction of military influence over the political center, concerns remained regarding the loyalty of the officer corps to the democratically elected government. Thus, as with the election of Chen Shui-bian in Taiwan, the election of former dissident Kim Dae-jung as president (1998–2002) was widely seen as marking the consolidation of civilian dominance in politics. Not only did the military abstain from interfering with Kim's election, they also acquiesced to the new president's more conciliatory stance toward North Korea (Saxer 2004: 386).

In the Southeast Asian nations, the results of reforms in these two areas of civilian control have been mixed. In Indonesia, abolishing military representation in parliament, and especially in subnational administrative positions, and revoking the military's *dwifungsi* (dual-function) doctrine were key demands of the democracy movement. Once the power struggle between the regime and the democratization movement was decided, military leaders remained neutral throughout the transfer of power and repeatedly stressed that they had no desire to interfere with the reform process. Under pressure from pro-democracy groups, political parties, the media and reform-minded military officers, the military leadership officially replaced *dwifungsi* in 1999 with the so-called New Paradigm, which stipulated the formal separation of the police from the military, the suspension of the practice of promoting active-duty military personnel to nonmilitary posts, a reduction (and, in the end, abolition) of legislative representation of the armed forces, as well as the promise that military personnel would honor the principle of political neutrality (Rabasa and Haseman 2002: 25–31; Said 2006). In a highly symbolic act, the Indonesian military was renamed Tentara Nasional Indonesia (TNI, Armed Forces of Indonesia), which had been the Indonesian military's official name during the early years of the Republic.

Today, active-duty officers no longer hold political positions or staff the central government's bureaucracy. Reserved military representation in parliament was abolished in 2004, and active military officers have not been allowed to serve as cabinet ministers since 1999. While retired officers accounted for a significant part of Wahid's government (14 percent), this decreased to around 10 percent under Megawati and Yudhoyono (Croissant et al. forthcoming; cf. table 6). Most importantly, the number of retired military personnel in local government dropped from 80 percent in the early 1970s to below 10 percent in 2010 (ibid.). The military has also all but lost its ability to influence local and provincial elections through the support of local commanders for particular political candidates (Mietzner 2009: 347).

Table 6. Military Officers in the Cabinet, Legislature, and Governor Posts in Indonesia (1967–2014)

Regime	Retired officers in the cabinet (%)	Retired officers in the legislature (%)	Active-duty officers serving as governor (%)
Suharto and Habibie (1967–1999)	31.3[*]	17.3[†]	43.8
Wahid (1999–2001)	14.8	8.5	0
Megawati (2001–2004)	9.8	8.5	0
Yudhoyono (2004–2009)	9.2	3.1	0
Yudhoyono (2009–2014)	9.4	2.1	0

Sources: Sebastian and Iisingdarsah 2011; author's calculations based on data from Kepres 1998, 1999, 2000, 2004, 2007, 2009; Jakarta Post 1999, 2000, 2001a, 2001b, 2004, 2009.
[*] 1968–1999; [†] 1971–1999.

While military influence in policymaking at the national level seems to be marginal, military commanders still influence decision making at the local level by diverting funds that would otherwise be available for civilian purposes (Jansen 2008: 446). A lack of coordination of military political activities by the TNI command has prevented the military from gaining any meaningful share of the decision-making power that has been moved to the local and provincial levels during decentralization (Honna 2006; Mahroza 2009). Remaining problems include the unfinished reforms of the territorial command structure and the thorny issue of military businesses, especially the additional income generated by military units and individual military personnel (see Mietzner 2009, 2011).

In the Philippines, the demise of the Marcos regime in February 1986—facilitated by intramilitary conflicts and the military's refusal to crack down on mass protests—set the stage for contestation between radicalized military factions and civilian elites. After coming into office, President Corazon Aquino made bold moves to change the direction of Philippine politics, retiring "overstaying generals," signing ceasefires with the communist insurgents and the Moro National Liberation Front, harboring leftist advisers in the presidential office, and establishing a human rights commission to investigate and publicize military abuses (Selochan 1998).

These policies triggered a series of seven abortive coups, staged by the Reform Armed Forces Movement and other radical factions such as Soldiers for the Filipino People and the Young Officers' Union (see Tiglao 1990). The last coup attempt, in December 1989, might have succeeded if not for US intervention. It was only when a reshuffle of the military leadership brought the AFP under the control of Chief-of-Staff Fidel Ramos, and after the president abandoned most of her reformist policies, that the rogue elements within AFP could be marginalized (Hedman 2001).

Compared with the first chaotic years of the Aquino administration, President Fidel Ramos (1992–1998) provided for more stable civil-military relations. As a former senior military officer, Ramos retained the support of most of the AFP officer corps. In order to prevent other coups, he promoted loyal officers to key military positions and recruited retired military officers to important posts in the national bureaucracy, the government, and two of the most profitable state enterprises (Gloria 2003; PCIJ 2011). This, however, had an ambiguous impact on civil-military relations. On the one hand, co-opting Ramos' faction in the military and encouraging military officers to run for office strengthened the president's personal authority and reduced the military's disposition to intervene (Hutchcroft 2000: 243). On the other hand, it increased the AFP's influence on policymaking and elite recruitment. Furthermore, it set an example for following governments, which in their efforts to protect the civilian administration against coup threats continued to appoint supporters to key military commands and military leaders to high government positions (Gloria 2003: 28–29).

While seemingly strengthening military compliance in the short run, this approach had a detrimental effect on civilian control in the long run, perpetuating and increasing the politicization of the officer corps and promoting political activism by the military. This was clearly demonstrated in 2001, when AFP senior commanders supported Vice President Gloria Macapagal-Arroyo and joined a popular uprising against President Joseph Estrada. Estrada's fall symbolized the military's rise as a moderating power in Philippine politics (Landé 2001). It is thus not surprising that the Arroyo government (2001–2010) was repeatedly battered by military adventurism (Hutchcroft 2008). In order to keep the military's loyalty, Arroyo had to court military favor, paying the rank and file with subsidized housing, increased benefits, and pay raises.

Distributing promotions and employing a revolving-door policy in appointing generals to the chief of staff position (with a total of 12 chiefs in 9 years), Arroyo surrounded herself with favored high commanders. During her administration, the practice of appointing scores of retired military officers to the country's strategic executive offices and civilian bureaucracy, which had begun under the Ramos administration (1992–1998), became endemic (Hernandez and Kraft 2010; Tordecilla 2011). The co-optation of military officers into government posts greatly strengthened "the influence and participation of the military in running the country's state affairs" (Gloria 2003: 33) and allowed it to exert considerable informal control over national and local administrations.

In contrast to the Philippines, where civil-military relations worsened after the transition to democracy, developments in Thailand actually seemed to indicate a decline of the Royal Thai Armed Forces' political power. The participation of active-duty officers in the cabinet and the representation of military officers in the Senate was greatly reduced after democratization (see figure 2). Furthermore, military prerogatives in foreign policy were cut and civilian authority over most other policy fields improved. With the adoption of a new constitution in 1997, the civilianization of the parliamentary system seemed to have made considerable progress. In fact, under the government of Prime Minister Thaksin Shinawatra (2001–2006), it seemed that the military's political power over elite recruitment and policymaking was finally contained (Croissant, Völkel, and Chambers 2011).

Figure 2. Military and Police Representation in Senate and Cabinet in Thailand (1932–2010)

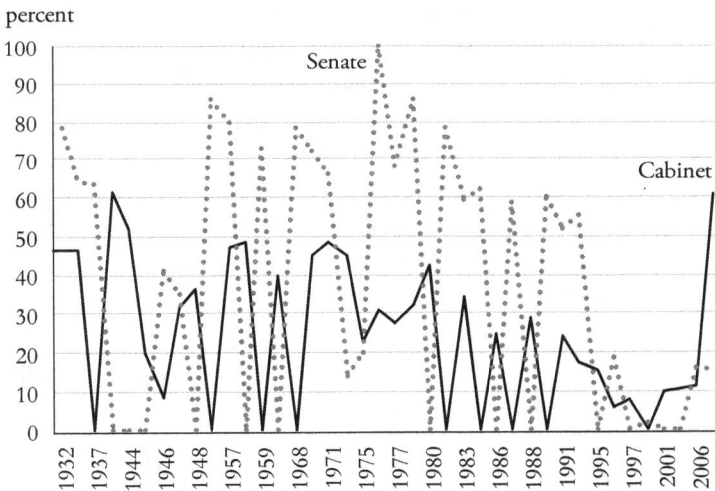

Source: Chambers 2010b.
Note: Numbers include retired and active-duty military and police officers.

The military coup of September 2006 reversed this trend. Following the military-appointed interim government (2006–2007), Thailand returned to civilian government. Under a democratic façade, however, the military continues to intervene in government formation and policy decisions whenever it believes it necessary for its own benefit or to defend the nation and the monarchy. Military leaders helped to bring down a pro-Thaksin government in 2008, and cobbled together another multiparty coalition under Prime Minister Abhisit (2008–2011).

The number of soldier-senators also rose again—from 2 percent in 2000 to 15.3 percent in 2008 (Chambers 2010b: 58–64).

Internal Security

Post-authoritarian developments in the area of internal security are diverse. Democratically elected governments successfully eliminated the military's internal security functions in Korea and Taiwan, but failed in Thailand and the Philippines. Indonesia holds a position somewhere along the continuum.

In Taiwan, military jurisdiction over civilians was abolished immediately after the lifting of martial law. In 1992, the Taiwan Garrison Command was dissolved, and its duties were transferred to civilian agencies. The civilian police took over the Command's law-enforcement functions, customs and immigration control were transferred to the Ministry of the Interior, and the ministry-level Government Information Office and the Ministry of Transport and Communication were tasked with censorship and media regulation (Hung, Mo, and Tuan 2003: 187–88).

In Korea, President Roh Tae-woo replaced the leadership of the military's domestic intelligence agency (the Defense Security Command) and renamed it the Military Security Command in an effort to distance himself from his former role as head of that agency. Both this agency and the Agency for National Security Planning withdrew their members from the National Assembly in 1988. A year later, the rank of the commander of the Military Security Command was downgraded from three-star to two-star general, the agency was significantly downsized, and its civilian surveillance bureau was abolished (Moon and Kang 1995: 185–86; Moon and Rhyu 2011). Subsequent administrations completed the separation of the military from internal security and domestic intelligence (Saxer 2004: 391). Finally, under President Kim Dae-jung (1998–2003) the intelligence service was put under a civilian directorate.

> *Under a democratic façade, the Thai military continues to intervene in government formation and policy decisions*

In contrast, civilians in the Southeast Asian countries were less successful in establishing firm control over this area. Given the long legacies of military involvement in counterinsurgency operations and persisting problems with ethno-religious separatism and political extremism, military officers have been reluctant to give up their involvement in internal security even after transition to democratic rule.

In Thailand, immediately following the end of the military regime in May 1992, the army was stripped of its control of the Capital Security Command, a constabulary military unit tasked with the restoration of public order during national emergencies (Murray 1996: 190–91). During the government of Thaksin Shinawatra (2001–2006), civilian influence in this decision-making area expanded considerably. The army's suppression of protests in rural areas and its role in the "war on drugs" in 2003 were decided by and remained under the personal control of Thaksin.

In 2005, the Thaksin administration passed the Decree on Government Administration in a State of Emergency, which allowed the prime minister to authorize a state of emergency, and it was applied to the provinces where the southern insurgency was raging. Thaksin also greatly reduced the power of the Internal Security Operations Command, the military's most powerful internal security force (Pasuk and Baker 2009: 328), and weakened the army's hold over the organization. Thaksin's further plans to restructure the Internal Security Operations Command and put it under direct control of the prime minister's office was thwarted by the 2006 coup (Avudh 2006).

Under the post-2006 political order, the maintenance of internal security and protection of state, nation, and monarchy from internal threats are clearly the exclusive domain of the military. The new Internal Security Act greatly strengthened the military's role in internal security and weakened parliamentary oversight. Among other things, it allows the military to arrest civilians without a warrant, and military personnel acting under the act are exempt from prosecution for human rights abuses (Chambers 2010b: 66–73). The junta, the so-called Council for Democratic Reform, created a number of special operation units tasked with quelling political protest. In addition, it re-established army control of the Internal Security Operations Command, giving the army more leeway in repressing political opposition, as during the Red Shirt demonstrations of 2009 and 2010. The military also exercises extensive control of the media, with 245 of the approximately 500 radio stations in military hands and a harsh Internet crime law enacted by the military-appointed Surayud government (cf. Chambers 2010a).

In the Philippines, President Corazon Aquino attempted to improve civilian oversight of the military's intelligence and constabulary functions. On paper, the new government introduced important reforms such as the establishment of a Human Rights Commission, the separation of police and armed forces, and new monitoring powers for Congress (Hernandez 2007: 86–87). The Philippine Constabulary, established in 1901 as a paramilitary police force, was removed from the Ministry of Defense and merged with the Integrated National Police into the new Philippine National Police in 1991. Moreover, the intelligence services were restructured, and responsibility for overseeing the activities of the National Intelligence and Security Authority was transferred to the president's national security advisor.

Nevertheless, major problems persisted. One of the thorniest was the precise division of labor between the police and the military, as 95 percent of the civilian police force consisted of personnel transferred from the Philippine Constabulary (Teodosio 1997: 31). Moreover, continuous military deployment in internal security operations weakened civilian control. A renewed communist insurgency in the early 2000s, and the Philippines' contribution to the "war on terror" in Mindanao and elsewhere, have led to an expansion of military prerogatives in counterinsurgency and counterterrorism without adequate civilian and parliamentary oversight (Hernandez 2002: 41; De Castro 2005: 17–18; Robles 2008; Santos 2010). Extrajudicial killings of left-wing political activists and harassment of civil society groups by military personnel or members of armed auxiliary groups under command of the AFP and the police, under the pretext of fighting communist-front organizations, continue with impunity (Hernandez 2007: 87; Hernandez and Kraft 2010: 126–29).[7]

In recent years, the Indonesian military (TNI) has lost much of its internal security role (Mietzner 2011). Most importantly, the Indonesian National Police was separated from the military in 1999 and, in 2009, civilians were for the first time put in charge of the Ministry of Home Affairs and the State Intelligence Agency (Mietzner 2011), formally giving civilians control over most aspects of counterterrorism. While President Yudhoyono put an active-duty general in charge of the State

Intelligence Agency in October 2011 (Witular 2011), and had earlier launched an initiative to expand the military's involvement in counterterrorism, civilians dominate this field and are increasingly able to triangulate with other sources the information on terrorist activities received through the military's territorial network (Mietzner 2009: 349, 351; Dharmono 2010). In day-to-day law enforcement, however, there are some gray zones in which military and police roles are poorly differentiated (Wandelt 2007; Pohlman 2010). This has at times resulted in local turf wars (which became less frequent after 2004), and deliberations on legislation to differentiate the two roles have failed (Human Rights Watch 2006: 66; Makaarim and Yunanto 2008: 60).

More conventional military tasks like counterinsurgency operations long remained problematic. When several simmering separatist and communal conflicts across the Indonesian archipelago erupted during and after democratization, the military was charged with putting them down, and civilians were unable to give any significant input or monitor the implementation of policies, let alone ensure the humane treatment of the local population. Despite some symbolic admissions of past human rights abuses, TNI also actively worked to undermine civilian peace initiatives in Aceh and what is now Timor-Leste

More conventional military tasks like counterinsurgency operations long remained problematic

during the early years of democratization (Miller 2009: 21), and combat operations continued unabated. Moreover, during these conflicts, operational control was usually exercised through the Coordinating Ministry for Politics and Security, in recent years usually controlled by a retired TNI commander (Dharmono 2010).

Under the government of President Yudhoyono, the military stopped openly challenging the government and finally accepted a peaceful resolution of the Aceh conflict in 2005. Before that, civilians had little choice but to blindly accept all military requests for the region (Mietzner 2009: 226, 229). Now, only the vagueness of relevant legislation, under-institutionalization of internal controls, and an unwillingness of civilians to implement a clear monitoring and sanctioning regimen hamper civilian control in this area.

National Defense and Military Organization

During the authoritarian era, defense policymaking and military organization were exclusive domains of the armed forces in Indonesia, South Korea, and Thailand. In Taiwan and the Philippines, military autonomy was more limited because of the preeminent political role of civilian presidents Chiang Ching-kuo and Ferdinand Marcos (Miranda 1992: 11; Swaine and Mulvenon 2001). However, even in these countries, civilian influence in external defense issues was unsystematic and lacked institutionalization. Given these traditions, post-authoritarian governments throughout the region found it equally difficult to establish full authority over national defense affairs.

In Taiwan, the institutionalization of civilian control in these areas was not accomplished until 2002, when the National Defense Act and the Organization Act of the Ministry of National Defense came into effect (Lo 2001). In this under-institutionalized civil-military environment, high-ranking officers were able to repeatedly prevail in conflicts of interest with President Lee Teng-hui—for instance, thwarting attempts for military reform and preventing the civilianization of the defense ministry.

Following high-profile procurement scandals in the early 1990s, some advances were made in enhancing legislative oversight of military affairs—for example, increasing the transparency of the procurement process and reducing the classified segment of the defense budget. Despite such progress, however, civilian governments found themselves unable to significantly increase their say in military affairs until the two defense laws were implemented (Kuehn 2008: 875–76). Following this legislation, the number of civilians in the defense ministry was increased, the command structures were reorganized, and defense policymaking was made more accountable (Chase 2005). Today, although the military still enjoys considerable clout in defense policymaking and the defense ministry remains under the leadership of a retired general, the military is able neither to dominate defense policy nor to bypass oversight and direction by the president and parliament.

In South Korea, reforms were equally cumbersome. The Roh Tae-woo administration failed to implement military reforms beyond a limited opening of defense spending to legislative oversight in 1991 (Croissant 2004: 371). Hence, defense policy remained a domain of active and retired military officers until President Kim Young-sam enforced the reduction of military autonomy. For example, in 1993, his administration investigated a series of procurement scandals as well as corruption cases involving a number of high-ranking officers. This not only put military issues under heightened public scrutiny but also set the precedent for more transparency and improved civilian oversight (Saxer 2004: 394).

Kim Young-sam also restructured the defense bureaucracy and strengthened the defense ministry vis-à-vis the general staff (Kim, Liddle, and Said 2006: 255). Such efforts notwithstanding, his government overall failed to implement military reforms in consultation with civilian and military experts as envisioned in the administration's Mid-term National Defense Plan for 1998–2002 (W. Kim 2008: 170).

After becoming president in 1998, Kim Dae-jung took an important step in expanding civilian control of defense affairs when he installed the civilian-dominated National Security Council as a presidential advisory body on security policymaking and coordination (Jun 2001: 134). Yet his administration did not completely succeed in reforming the military; its reform plan, drafted by a civilian-military committee, "was not carried out because of strong resistance from the army and the lack of budgetary resources due to the [1997 Asian] financial crisis" (W. Kim 2008: 170).

Nevertheless, when Roh Moo-hyun (2003–2008) was elected president, he was able to build on the preceding governments' achievements and did not need to deal with serious challenges from the armed forces. Instead, President Roh turned his attention to realizing a comprehensive defense and military reform—improving military cost-effectiveness and technological, organizational, and doctrinal modernization of the Korean armed forces in order to cope with the challenges of the "revolution in military affairs" in the early 21st century (ibid.: 162; Raska 2011).

Under Roh, the National Security Council became the primary defense decision-making agency, with the effect of reducing the military and the civilian defense bureaucracy to "bystanders when it comes to real influence in defense policy-making" (Bechtol 2005: 625). The new president also furthered the reform of the personnel management system and military education. Beginning in 2005, his administration introduced military political education and higher education for officers at civilian institutions and international training programs, and it reformed leadership principles in order to strengthen the acceptance of democratic civilian control (K. Kim 2009: 158).

Roh also continued a new style of personnel management and military promotions introduced by President Kim Dae-jung that was not based on favoritism or nepotism—as it had been under Park, Chun, Roh Tae-woo, and to some extent Kim Young-sam—but on institutionalized rules and procedures that opened career opportunities for military officers. Promotion criteria shifted from seniority, which had generally favored nepotism and favoritism, to a merit-based system initiated by Kim Dae-jung, which further strengthened the acceptance of democratic civilian control among military officers (Moon and Rhyu 2011).

In comparison with Taiwan and South Korea, civilians in Thailand made little progress in curtailing military autonomy or enforcing their authority over national defense policy. Even before the military coup of 2006, civilians had almost no influence on defense policymaking, leaving all national defense issues to the military. With regard to military organization, the military successfully shielded its autonomy from civilian influence and actively resisted civilian incentives to military reform.

> *In comparison with Taiwan and South Korea, civilians in Thailand made little progress in enforcing their authority over defense policy*

When Prime Minister Chuan Leekpai in 1997 became the first civilian defense minister in 20 years, he was unable to implement most military reforms in the way they were intended. For instance, plans to improve military efficiency and civilian oversight by reforming military promotion procedures, reorganizing the command structure, and cutting the vast number of generals without duties were blocked by military veto. Only in instances in which civilian incentives for defense reform corresponded with the military's own goals, for example in reducing troop strength, could civilians realize their plans (Ockey 2001: 198–203). Hence, at no time in the democratic period were civilians ever able to effectively steer core military and defense issues, such as the defense budget, weapons acquisition, arms deployment, force structure, and education and training.

After Thaksin became prime minister in February 2001, most efforts to extend civilian influence over defense affairs ended. In his attempt to secure military support, Thaksin gave the armed forces a free hand to manage their own internal affairs and summarily approved procurement plans and a steep increase in defense spending (McCargo and Ukrist 2005: 151–57). However, senior military promotions remained an important exception, as they became a tool for the prime minister to influence the military leadership.

The 2006 coup, unsurprisingly, did not contribute to improved civilian authority over military organization and defense policy. Rather, military officials informally pressured civilian governments to augment military budgets, and the military regained control over promotions and personnel management (Chambers 2010b: 76–82). Also, the civilianized National Security Council under the prime minister is paralleled by a military-dominated Defense Council in the Ministry of Defense, which creates institutional redundancies that undermine civilian control (ibid.: 73–76). Finally, although the civilian prime minister has the formal power to appoint senior military officers, in practice the military continues to select its leadership without significant civilian input (cf. Chambers 2010a). Even the newly elected (July 2011) pro-Thaksin government of Prime Minister Yinluck Shinawatra needed to put a military officer, General Yuttasak Sasiprapa, in charge of the Ministry of Defense.

In contrast, Indonesia has seen some progress in enhancing civilian influence and increasing transparency; however, the process included some temporary setbacks. President Wahid's attempt to promote reformist officers in order to foster their personal loyalty in 2001 had alienated the military leadership so much that they supported his impeachment and lent their support to his vice-president, who succeeded him in office. For the first time since the 1950s, Presidents Wahid and Megawati appointed civilian defense ministers, and in 2003 the defense ministry outlined the first ostensibly civilian official security threat assessment in a white paper. Other than this, however, the Wahid and Megawati governments failed to achieve substantial progress (BICC 2006: 2–4).

After Wahid's removal, the new president acquiesced to most military demands for autonomy, and day-to-day oversight by the defense ministry remained ineffective due to the lack of resources, institutions, and expertise (Wandelt 2007: 269). Even though it has always been headed by a civilian, the defense ministry to this day is overwhelmingly staffed with military officers, and the new post of deputy minister has recently been introduced, occupied by an influential active-duty military officer. This enables the military to "protect [its] corporate interests under a civilian minister" (Editors 2008: 87).

In September 2004, parliament did pass a law on the TNI that included several provisions related to military financing and prohibited military business activities. However, even though the president issued a decree in 2009 to take over military businesses it failed to include "the large bulk of TNI's assets" (Mietzner 2011: 275) consisting of foundations and cooperatives. Similarly, there were no serious attempts to curb the involvement of individual soldiers in moonlighting or criminal activities (ibid.). In addition, the government has so far been unwilling or unable to push for a reform of military tribunals that would put crimes committed by off-duty military personnel under the jurisdiction of civilian courts. Despite public presidential appeals to the military to accept a bill to this effect, the military-controlled Ministry of Defense managed to delay the issue long enough to move it off the table (Braun 2008: 181). In contrast, the Indonesian government has started to reform military education and introduce courses to increase awareness of democratic norms and human rights, starting with the upper ranks, and civilians are beginning to formulate a clear set of promotion criteria (Hadi 2010).

Historically, national defense had never been a top priority for policymakers in the Philippines. Due to the comprehensive defense agreement with the United States and the military's focus on internal security, civilians had no incentive to build the institutional framework to formulate defense policies and to control the military's internal organization (Selochan 1998: 62–64). Furthermore, Marcos had abolished all formerly existing institutions and oversight instruments, leaving his personal influence as the only civilian means to control defense and military policy (Hedman 2001: 172–80).

The 1987 constitution laid a solid foundation for increasing civilian participation in defense issues, making the president the commander-in-chief of the armed forces and conferring on Congress the power to appoint high-ranking officers, decide the defense budget, and investigate military affairs (Hernandez 2002: 33–34). After the 2003

Oakwood mutiny, in which 300 officers occupied a mall and hotel complex in Makati city to protest alleged corruption in the Arroyo government, the administration took some cosmetic steps to initiate security sector reforms. For example, President Arroyo appointed a civilian secretary of defense and a full-time security advisor (Hernandez 2005: 4).

These institutional changes have not significantly increased civilian influence in defense decision making and military affairs, however, as the military still dominates all defense-related agencies, including genuinely civilian bodies. Former military officers make up the bulk of Department of Defense, National Security Council, and National Intelligence Coordinating Agency personnel, as these agencies lack civilian experts (Hernandez 2002: 43). Therefore, all major programs for military reform and modernization have been designed by the military, which has then pushed for congressional approval (De Castro 2005).

Neither the failure of the AFP Modernization Program (passed by Congress in 1997) nor the missed opportunity to implement far-reaching reforms after the mutiny were the result of military resistance to civilian influence. In fact, Congress had repeatedly asserted itself against military demands for higher defense budgets and force modernization (De Castro 2005: 7–11; 2010). However, since 1986, elected officials in the legislative and executive branches of government have been unwilling to reduce their connections with and reliance on the military establishment and to professionalize the armed forces. Among other things, this would entail an end to arbitrary military appointments and promotions, militarization of the state machinery, corruption, and politically motivated interference in military matters. Professionalization would also mean that civilians would lose the military as an important source of political support. Given that the accumulation of resources and the establishment of patronage networks in the military are "two crucial components of [elected civilians'] control over local and national politics" (De Castro 2005: 18), civilians have no incentive to strive for greater professionalism of the military or to keep it out of politics.

Table 7 illustrates the balance between civilian and military authority as of December 2010. It reveals that civilian control in East Asia is a complex phenomenon that defies generalization. While democratization has brought major changes to civil-military relations in all five countries, only in Taiwan and South Korea have civilians succeeded in firmly establishing control over all five decision-making areas. In both countries, the chances of military intervention in politics appear to have become remote. In contrast, in Indonesia, and especially in the Philippines and Thailand, the military has guarded its prerogatives much more successfully in the post-authoritarian era. However, given the initial conditions in 1998, the Indonesian military's subordination to civilian authority is surprisingly solid. Although major problems remain, especially the need to dismantle the military's territorial command structure and to place its economic activities under civilian oversight, it is increasingly unlikely that the military will re-establish its powerful earlier role.

Table 7. Decision-Making Power, Civilians and the Military (2010)

	Thailand	Philippines	Indonesia	Taiwan	South Korea
Elite recruitment	Gray	Gray	White	White	White
Public policy	Gray	Gray	White	White	White
Internal security	Black	Gray	Gray	White	White
National defense	Black	Gray	Gray	White	White
Military organization	Black	Gray	Gray	White	White

Black = The military dominates decision making. Gray = Significant limits on civilian decision making exist, but the military does not dominate. White = Civilians dominate decision making.

Since 1986, civil-military relations in the Philippines have permitted formal civilian control over all five decision-making areas. Informally, however, military officers have kept their influence over internal security and military internal affairs, and even expanded their roles into elite recruitment and national defense. Thailand, on the other hand, is a clear case of failed civilian control. The democratic façade of the post-2007 parliamentary system notwithstanding, civilian governments are unable to exert substantial control over the military. Many observers agree that, in principle, the military could veto almost any political decision (see Chambers 2010a; Freedom House 2011; Bertelsmann Stiftung 2012).

Factors that Enable or Hinder Civilian Control

Why did civilians succeed in gaining control over the military in South Korea, Taiwan, and to some extent Indonesia, while they failed in Thailand and the Philippines? In the literature on civil-military relations, there is little agreement on what creates stable, institutionalized civilian control in new democracies. Samuel Huntington's theory of military professionalism, outlined in *The Soldier and the State* (1957), has long been considered the "dominant theoretical paradigm" (Feaver 2003: 7). However, several scholars have recognized major problems with this approach, and many innovative theoretical approaches have since been developed.[8] As Kuehn and Lorenz (2011) note, most of these can be grouped into two categories.

Theories in the first category focus on the environment of civil-military relations. They argue that civilian control ultimately depends on one or more structural or environmental factors—the political values of the armed forces or of society (cf. Stepan 1988; Fitch 1998; Loveman 1999; Mares 1998), the internal or international threat environment in which civil-military relations are embedded (Desch 1999), a society's level of socioeconomic development, political mobilization, and institutionalization (Alagappa 2001b), the institutional legacies of the authoritarian regime and the path to transition, or the institutional setup of the state (Agüero 1995; Pion-Berlin 1997).

Theories in the second category (for example, Hunter 1997; Geddes 1999; Trinkunas 2005) do not refer to structural factors but explain military retreat to the barracks and the subsequent emergence or failure of civilian control as the outcome of strategic interactions between civilian and military actors.

A key difference between the two categories is the relative importance they attach to structure and agency (Kuehn and Lorenz 2011). Theories in the first category confront the problem that environmental variables—macro-social and macro-political factors, political institutions or ideational factors—doubtless affect civil-military relations, but they only become relevant through the concrete actions of civilian and military actors. In other words, there is no direct causal connection between structures, ideas, or institutions and the establishment or failure of civilian control. At the same time, agency does not take place in a vacuum, but is influenced at least to some degree by structure—that is, a more-or-less large collection of more-or-less stable environmental factors, be they the results of prior human agency, such as the institutional legacies of the authoritarian regime, or the material surroundings in which the interactions between civilians and the military take place, such as the international system. Theoretical frameworks in the second category, however, almost completely neglect the influence of the environment or structural contexts on the agency of civilian or military actors.

The challenge is to integrate structure and agency into a coherent framework (ibid; see also Pion-Berlin 2011).[9] To this end, Croissant, Völkel, and Chambers (2011) have suggested an understanding of civilian control over the military in new democracies (or the lack thereof) as the outcome of a complex interplay between structural factors and human agency. Building on insights from Harold Trinkunas (2005), they focus on the political entrepreneurship and strategic actions of civilians: the crafting of civilian control in new democracies ultimately depends on the ability of civilians to dissolve military prerogatives remaining from the authoritarian period and introduce new institutions that ensure the supremacy of civilians in political decision making. These strategies aim at co-opting, recruiting, appeasing, or intimidating military officers into supporting the enforcement and institutionalization of civilian control (see also Trinkunas 2005: 10).

> *The challenge is to integrate structure and agency into a coherent framework*

However, while it is ultimately the conduct of political actors that explains the outcome of civil-military interactions, the environmental context presents those actors with resources and opportunities (see also Hay and Wincott 1998). In order for civilians to successfully implement strategies of control over the military, they must have sufficient resources. Therefore, actors will have to take into consideration the environment in which their strategy is carried out, as the choice and its outcome depend on the constraints and resources at their disposal.

Civilian politicians can develop different strategies to tame the military within a given context, with each strategy requiring different resources. Contexts themselves are "strategically selective"—given a specific context, only certain courses of action are likely to realize the actors' intentions (Hay 2002: 127).

Following Trinkunas's argument, Croissant, Kuehn, et al. (2011) assume that the success or failure of civilian control depends to a large extent on the political skills of civilians: although a given outcome is strategically selected for, it is by no means inevitable, and unintended consequences may be frequent. While we observe systematically structured outcomes, political entrepreneurship—that is, the ability of politicians to act as "strategic, self-activated innovators who recast political institutions and governing relationships" (Sheingate 2007: 13)—remains crucial.

Structural Factors

This study argues that both structure and agency are important to explain post-transitional civil-military relations in all five countries. Croissant, Kuehn, et al. (2011) discuss the relationship between several structural factors and the strategy choices of civilians. However, they do not offer specific hypotheses on which variables will precisely relate to choices and their outcomes. They argue that the effect of an individual factor depends on the perception of actors and their skillfulness, political will, preferences, and adaptability. Moreover, different factors interact, alternately reinforcing each other's effects and cancelling them out. Nevertheless, a careful analysis of civil-military relations in East Asia suggests that at least three sets of variables deserve closer scrutiny (for more details, see also Croissant and Kuehn 2009, 2011b; Croissant et al. forthcoming).

First, institutional legacies of the authoritarian era and the mode of transition to democracy seem to matter for the success or failure of post-transition civilian control. From this perspective, Taiwan stands out as a country that already had a relatively strong degree of civilian authority over the military before transition started. Other Asian countries have not been so fortunate. The armed forces in Korea and Thailand possessed strong traditions of political interventionism. In the Philippines, the tradition of civilian control—introduced by the United States in the 1930s, cherished as an integral part of officers' education and training at the Philippine Military Academy, and more or less accepted by AFP officers after 1946—eroded under the influence of President Marcos's authoritarian government (cf. McCoy 2000).

Furthermore, the mode of transition in the Philippines facilitated the pathologies that resulted from the de-institutionalization of civil-military relations during the Marcos years. Similarly, the specific modes of transitions to democracy in Indonesia and Thailand left many features of military supremacy untouched. However, legacies of authoritarian rule do not predetermine the post-transitional patterns of civil-military relations; rather, they are filtered through the specific path to democracy (Agüero 1995: 28–30), as is demonstrated by the trajectory of civil-military relations in South Korea and Indonesia.

A second factor that seems important for the development of civil-military relations in East Asia is the threat environment. The course of civil-military relations in Thailand, Indonesia, and the Philippines gives credence to the argument that "challenging internal threat environments, combined with few external threats, can seriously undermine civilian control of the military" (Desch 1999: 111–12). Undoubtedly, internal conflicts represented the most serious threat to territorial integrity and national security in all three countries. In the Philippines, persistent internal conflict made civilians dependent on the military and thus inhibited the reduction of military prerogatives in internal security and other areas. In addition, the inability of elected governments to provide peaceful means of settling social conflicts undermined the legitimacy of civilian actors and democratic institutions, providing a breeding ground for the extension of military influence and interventionism.

Similarly, in Thailand, the expanding insurgency in the south made many ranking Thai military officials uneasy about the Thaksin government's handling of the conflict. Although this was not the main reason for the 2006 military coup, it certainly contributed to it by further alienating a segment of the military from the civilian leadership (Croissant 2007).

Conversely, over the past 10 years or so, armed secessionist threats and communal and religious violence in Indonesia have drastically declined, and internal stability has improved significantly. While this has certainly strengthened civilian authority and government legitimacy (cf. Mietzner 2011), it remains unclear how much of this change in the internal threat environment is really reflected in the military perception of its mission, role, and relationship with civilian authorities.

In Korea and Taiwan, the combination of clearly defined external threats (North Korea and the People's Republic of China, respectively) and the absence of domestic insurgencies have facilitated civilian control, reducing the military's role as provider of regime stability and allowing for a successful cutback of its formerly pronounced internal security role. This has motivated the military to focus on its core function, defense against the external enemy. Finally, the ending of the Cold War and the relaxation of the inter-Korean relationship "allowed the civilian leadership to undertake a bold move to restructure the military for the direction of strengthening the civilian control of the military" (Moon and Rhyu 2011).

Third, the empirical evidence indicates an almost circular relationship between civilian control of the military and democratic consolidation: the degree of civilian control affects prospects for democratic consolidation, which in turn affect prospects for civilian control. With peaceful democratic transitions driven by a combination of civil society, international pressure, and elite negotiations, followed by almost a decade of relative political stability and continued economic growth, South Korea and Taiwan have become shining examples of "third wave" democratization. This is not to say that there were no rivalries or conflicts among civilians in both countries or that these did not have a negative impact on military reforms.

> *There appears to be an almost circular relationship between civilian control of the military and democratic consolidation*

One example that shows the detrimental effects of deep polarization between government and opposition parties in Taiwan is the intense debate over Taiwan's arms procurement program under President Chen Shui-bian (2000–2008; see Kuehn 2008). In South Korea, there have been serious debates over North Korean politics under Kim Dae-jung and, of course, the failed impeachment trial against Roh Moon-hyun, which also had the potential to shake civilian-military relations (W. Kim 2008: 157). Overall, however, civilians in both countries provided effective government, and almost no one in political or civil society questioned the legitimacy of democracy and civilian government. In such circumstances, establishing civilian control was much easier than in Thailand and the Philippines, where civilian political institutions are weak and the legitimacy of the democratic regime remains contested. Both countries have experienced popular uprisings against elected governments. In Thailand, the result was a full-scale coup in 2006; in the Philippines, the military-backed civilian takeover of 2001 has been described as a civil society coup (Arugay 2011; Thompson 2011).

Indonesia, by contrast, has seen no major extraconstitutional threat to the government since 1999. Obviously, there are many weaknesses in Indonesian democracy, particularly in terms of government efficiency, rule of law, and collusion among elites (Aspinall and Mietzner 2010). Despite these shortcomings, the stabilization of the civilian polity has helped to marginalize the armed forces from the power center. Perhaps most significantly, Indonesian democracy benefits from a comparatively strong civil society, a well-institutionalized political party system (cf. Croissant and Völkel 2012; Thompson 2011; Hicken and Kuhonta 2011), and inclusionary coalition politics among Indonesia's political elite. These create opportunities for civilians to gain the upper hand in decisions on the role of the military in the new democracy (Croissant 2011; Mietzner 2011). Furthermore, conditional civilian control in Indonesia was supported by the democratic regime's ability to produce and maintain public support, civilian consensus on the need to keep the military out of politics, and an active civil society that provided politicians with additional monitoring of and information about military affairs (ibid; Croissant, Völkel, and Chambers 2011).

In the Philippines and Thailand, reality is rather different. The military's role in the downfall of President Estrada in 2001 had far-reaching consequences for civil-military relations in the Philippines. Carolina Hernandez (2005) not only argues that the events of January 2001 and the Oakwood Mutiny of 2003 set back the process of democratizing civil-military relations in the Philippines, but also shows that civil-military relations remained essentially the same as prior to 1986. This was characterized by an enlarged military role—including responsibility for responding to domestic armed threats to the government and carrying out national development functions. Fragile political legitimacy of the incumbent administration, weak civilian oversight institutions, poor socioeconomic conditions, and armed conflicts provided the foundations for an increased military involvement in government (Hernandez and Kraft 2010; Arugay 2010).

The crisis of democracy is particularly evident in Thailand. However, the resurrection of the military as the dominant political force in 2006 seems to be a consequence rather than a cause of democratic stress in Thailand. Even before the recent coup, the first in 15 years, Thai democracy showed severe symptoms of erosion and steady weakening by those elected to lead it (McCargo and Ukrist 2005). Instead of consolidating the democratic gains of the 1990s, the Thaksin years were characterized by increasingly authoritarian governance and deepening polarization between opponents and supporters of the government, which clearly indicated the existence of strong centrifugal forces in the country (Thitinan 2008).

The failure of democracy was a consequence of the incapacity of the political system to accommodate these social and political tensions. The main shortcoming has been the weakly organized social bases for mass parties and the lack of adequate representation of the interests of the urban working class and rural voters. The legitimacy of the political aspirations and preferences of those segments of Thai society had never been fully accepted by the political elites. Thaksin and his Thai Rak Thai party had attempted to fill this vacuum since the late 1990s. When Thaksin menaced the prerogatives of royalist military personnel, the palace, and the Bangkok elites, these groups formed a civilian-military coup coalition against him (Croissant 2008; Thompson 2011).

The Role of Agency

While structural factors have influenced processes and outcomes in all five countries, the case studies show that the agency of civilian decision makers plays an important role in accounting for the diverging patterns of civil-military relations. Strategic action, prioritization, and careful timing by civilians, who took advantage of opportunities to restructure civil-military relations, have enabled Korea, Taiwan, and Indonesia to overcome past legacies of military intervention in politics. In all three countries, civilians strategically chose their actions to maximize their leverage over the armed forces.

Strategic action also explains some of the differences between the cases. In Korea, President Kim Young-sam aggressively pushed the military out of politics by purging the politicized members of the officer corps who had dominated the country's political system since the first coup in 1961. Kim, however, benefited from several factors that provided the political and institutional resources necessary for the success of such strategies:

- Existing monitoring mechanisms within the military organization effectively prevented the military from intervening in governmental affairs and were conducive to civilian monitoring and control of the military and its eventual depoliticization (Moon and Rhyu 2011).

- Consolidated and unified presidential authority over the promotions of high-ranking generals gave Kim Young-sam the institutional resources to purge the military without interference from the legislature or the military.[10]

- Factional tensions within the military could be utilized to balance military power and strengthen the president's position vis-à-vis the military. As a result of the systematic discrimination against non-Hanahoe officers during the Chun Doo-hwan regime, the vast majority of military officers had nothing to gain from the status quo and therefore no incentive to defend Hanahoe (I. Kim 2008: 155–56).

In Taiwan, the successful institutionalization of civilian control was also influenced by legacies of civil-military relations under the authoritarian regime, which, however, did not uniformly benefit the civilian government. On the one hand, there was a robust tradition of military subordination to the president and the party elite, so that civilians did not have to engage the military in a prolonged struggle for dominance in elite recruitment. On the other hand, the complete absence of functional institutions of oversight and control over defense and military affairs meant that civilians had to establish such mechanisms from scratch. Hence, institutionalizing control in these areas was a gradual and protracted process.

Civilians succeeded in pushing back the remnants of the authoritarian era by a variety of strategies, in which they refrained from open confrontation with the conservative military leadership. Early in his term, President Lee Teng-hui (1986–2000) realized that as a civilian without a military career background he could only overcome the Kuomintang generals' criticism of democratization by addressing the military's concerns. Therefore, he adopted a soft approach toward the military and refrained from intervening in its internal affairs; instead, he delegated a high degree of authority to politically trusted officers. Particularly important was the presidential prerogative of personnel promotion and retirement, which was used extensively by President Lee (and also by Chen Shui-bian) to put loyal officers and supporters of their political vision into the military leadership (Chen 2010).

This was possible due to a combination of environmental factors that provided civilians with the resources to cut back the military's political prerogatives, and weakened the military's incentives and capacity to frustrate the extension of civilian control. Following the historical change in government, President Chen Shui-bian followed Lee Teng-hui's example and refrained from radical changes during his first term in office. Having won the election by only a small margin, and faced with a parliament controlled by the opposition, he simply did not have the political resources to initiate a large-scale change in civil-military relations. Instead, he strengthened the role of civilians within the National Security Council (Chen 2010: 14); especially during his second term, he relied on his promotion powers to recruit loyal officers into the military leadership (Tzeng 2009: 162–63; W. Lee 2007: 125; Chen 2010).

Successes in securing civilian control in post-authoritarian Indonesia resulted mainly from the prudent approach to the military by which civilian governments were able to overcome existing disadvantages in civil-military relations, including the entrenched traditions of the military's political influence. In contrast to South Korea, civilian presidents in Indonesia mostly relied on softer maneuvering, and kept the military at bay by skillfully recruiting supporters into the higher echelons of military leadership. This, however, hampered the stronger institutionalization of civilian control and perpetuated the established mechanisms of informally regulated civil-military relations.

First, the military accepted reforms only because interim President Habibie (1998–1999) had cultivated strong personal relations with controversial senior military leaders such as General Wiranto (Kim, Liddle, and Said 2006: 257–61). Second, the military itself decided on the scope and contents of depoliticization and the redefinition of its political role. The New Paradigm, for example, was conceived and implemented by so-called intellectual generals (including the current president, Yudhoyono), with civilians playing hardly any role in the process (Honna 2003: 164–67). Furthermore, Habibie's successors did not follow up on his first steps, so that under Presidents Wahid (1999–2001) and Megawati (2001–2004) little progress in strengthening civilian control was made. Rather, Megawati's policy of relying on personal connections with the military leadership and promoting trusted officers to government positions contributed to a return of military influence in policymaking and implementation (Kingsbury 2003: 240). As a result, executive initiatives for civil-military reform ground to a halt, and parliament had to step up in order to save ongoing efforts. Existing problems in military reform in Indonesia seem to be caused more by civilian unwillingness (or inability) to press for substantial reform than by the military's resistance to civilian attempts to reduce its influence in political and civilian affairs.

The cases of the Philippines and Thailand show that civilian agency does not necessarily lead to strong civilian control. Presidents Fidel Ramos (1992–1998) and Gloria Macapagal Arroyo (2001–2010) assigned their loyalists in the military to posts in government-owned corporations, special economic zones, and two of the government's biggest revenue-generating agencies: the Department of Transportation and Communications and the Bureau of Customs. Under the Arroyo and Ramos governments, former military officers also were in charge of the government's fifth biggest revenue earner, the Land Transportation Office (Gloria 2003).

> *Civilian agency does not necessarily lead to strong civilian control*

In addition, politicians consolidated their personal control over centralized patronage networks and co-opted military officers into the civilian sphere, which allowed them to marginalize the most radical military factions, and in turn enabled officers to pursue their corporate and private interests. This strategy of co-option has been partially successful. While it helped to protect civilian administrations against coups and destabilization, it continued the politicization of the AFP, contributed to the militarization of the government apparatus and the decision-making process, and gave the AFP wide-ranging influence in key policy areas.

Furthermore, even the seemingly positive effects of the administrations' appeasement and compensation strategies were helpful only in the short term. The failure to arrest, try, and imprison suspected mutineers and coup plotters delivered the message that in the Philippines, military adventurism would not be dealt with severely (Gloria 1999). Furthermore, even though the AFP's involvement in extrajudicial killings of civilians is well known and repeatedly reported on by government commissions, human rights groups, and the UN special rapporteur, not a single military service member accused of violating human rights has been successfully prosecuted (Hutchcroft 2008: 147).

Similarly, the case of Thailand demonstrates that keeping the military out of politics is only half of the challenge. The other half is to protect the military from becoming a vehicle for the partisan interests of government leaders. Immediately after becoming prime minister, Thaksin began to transform the military into his personal power base by granting it a large range of old and new prerogatives. In an attempt to appease and co-opt the military, Thaksin repeatedly interfered with military promotions, assigning supporters, family members, and military academy classmates to key military positions (Ukrist 2008: 127). At the same time, he increased the military budget, lifted the embargo on military procurements that had been in place since the 1997 financial crisis, and summarily approved the military's procurement list for 2005–2013 (Scarpello 2005; McCargo and Ukrist 2005: 134–57).

In addition, the lower house—despite the fact that it had the formal right to scrutinize defense policy—"has not taken any steps to empower itself as an informed and authoritative force in military affairs" (Surachart 2001: 88–89). This was in part because members of parliament did not have the expertise, resources, and institutional capacity in military and security affairs (ibid.). More important, however, there was no incentive for them to develop the competence to conduct debates on military affairs. In the short run, meddling with the military's internal affairs and co-opting generals rather than confronting them worked well for the prime minister, as it enhanced his leverage over the armed forces. In the end, however, it had disastrous consequences for civilian rule in Thailand. Many officers saw Thaksin's efforts to co-opt the military as a threat to the unity and integrity of the armed forces and as a challenge to the monarchy (Ukrist 2008: 139). In the eyes of the putschists, the September 2006 coup was a last-ditch defense against the consolidation of Thaksin's personal regime, which would have neutralized the military as an autonomous political force.

Conclusion

Three conclusions can be drawn from this analysis. First, civilian control means more than the absence of a military coup or other open military intervention. By distinguishing different decision-making areas, a systematic and nuanced analysis of the different states of civil-military relations and their development over time can be drawn. This makes it possible to differentiate not only between cases but also within cases. This is particularly important for countries in which the balance of decision-making power between civilians and military personnel varies in different areas of civil-military relations, as is true of Thailand, Indonesia, and the Philippines. Taking these differences into account, it becomes clear not only that the democratizing states in East Asia have different patterns of civil-military relations but that there is much variation within each country.

Such differentiations notwithstanding, it seems fair to conclude that South Korea achieved civilian control after Kim Young-sam was elected in 1993 as the first genuinely civilian president in over 30 years. Today, democratically elected authorities and institutions in Korea effectively control all matters of civil-military relations, including mission profiles, personnel management, procurement, and organization. Similarly, in Taiwan, civilian control is firmly established and the prospects are good that it will survive any future political crisis. In Indonesia, civilian control is also rather stable, as the TNI today has influence neither on the selection of the political leadership nor on the making and implementation of national policies. However, President Yudhoyono's control over the military remains under-institutionalized and mostly depends on his network of patronage and loyalty inside the military. Hence, civilian control over the Indonesian military "remains vulnerable to possible fluctuations in the quality of Indonesia's young democracy as well as the distinct personalities of its top leaders" (Mietzner 2011).

The experiences of Taiwan, Korea, and to some degree Indonesia contrast with the outright failure of civilian control in Thailand and the prolonged crisis of civil-military relations in the Philippines. In Thailand, elected governments have thus far not been able to end military domination in any of the five areas discussed above. The military acts as a self-proclaimed guardian of king and nation. Even after the end of direct military rule in late 2007, military personnel have continued to exert great decision-making power far beyond defense and military organization.

What explains the difference between Thailand and the Philippines? Why is it that in the Philippines military rebels so far have failed to topple the government, while in Thailand they succeeded? The answer to this question seems clear: Despite the many failings of democracy in the Philippines, most civilian factions, elites and rank-and-file citizens alike, believe that a military overthrow of the executive would be illegitimate. This is one of the main reasons that the Philippine military (in contrast to its peers in Thailand) "does not really seek to capture political power for itself (despite all the instances of attempted coups), and instead institutionally (through the upper ranks of the military leadership) aligns itself with certain political factions" (Hernandez and Kraft 2010: 130). This symbiotic relationship (ibid.) between civilian and military elites allows civilian rule to survive. In Thailand, however, there has been no civilian anti-coup consensus. On the contrary: in 2006, segments of the Thai population and elites, including some social activists and civilian politicians, formed (presumably with support from royalist circles) a military-civilian coalition to overthrow the civilian government of Prime Minister Thaksin Shinawatra, thereby granting legitimacy to the military under certain circumstances to act as "moderator" (Nordlinger 1977).

Second, agency akin to what Adam Sheingate (2007) calls political entrepreneurship is crucial. To overcome challenges and obstacles in institutionalizing civilian authority over the military, civilian agents must take advantage of the opportunities and resources provided by structural contexts and use them to develop appropriate strategies for controlling the military. While agents in different Asian countries develop different strategies, the examples of Korea and, to a lesser extent, Indonesia suggest that personnel management and promotion policies, divide-and-conquer strategies, civilian acquiescence, and the legitimization of civilian control are the most crucial elements in what may be labeled as creative and shifting combinations of soft and robust control strategies.

Civilian agents must take advantage of the opportunities and resources provided by structural contexts

On the other hand, as the experiences of South Korea, Indonesia, and Taiwan demonstrate, "flexible opportunism" (Padgett and Ansell 1993) on the part of civilians can also mean not pursuing too much too soon in civil-military relations, including the prosecution of crimes committed during the authoritarian era, as long as the distribution of political power favors the military. In South Korea, for example, transitional justice was not tackled until almost a decade after the transition to democracy, while Taiwan is among the few countries in the third wave of democratization in which transitional justice has never been on the political agenda (Wu 2005: 6).

Third, it is not sufficient to focus exclusively or predominantly on the military side. All cases analyzed in detail in this paper suggest that civil-military reforms in new democracies are made more difficult by a lack of civilian security and decision-making infrastructure, weak electoral incentives for civilians to learn about the political management of the armed forces, and the lack of civilian capacity to manage the security sector. Thai Prime Minister Thaksin's handling of civil-military relations between 2001 and 2006 illustrates the importance, not only of keeping the military out of politics, but also of protecting the military from exploitation for partisan purposes by civilian leaders (Watts 2002).

These findings make it possible to draw some tentative conclusions about possible future trajectories in civil-military relations in East Asia. The Philippines and Thailand will most likely be plagued by military assertion and a lack of civilian control for some time. Given the deep entrenchment of the military in their political systems, the manifold problems they face in consolidating democracy, the persistence of internal conflict, and the limited capacity of civilian governments to pursue military reforms, civilians are unlikely to be sufficiently willing or able to confront the military and diminish its influence in the political arena. Significant extension of civilian control of the security sector in these two countries remains unlikely.

For Taiwan and South Korea, the picture is much less grim. Both countries have made significant progress in establishing and institutionalizing civilian control over the military. Today, the civilian governments have all the institutional mechanisms and instruments they need to keep the military out of politics and to effectively steer defense and military policy. The factors that helped enable these developments during and after the transition to democracy are likely to persist: both countries are now consolidated liberal democracies, and democratic principles are internalized and shared by the overwhelming majority of the population. Most importantly, survey data show that there is no support for a larger military role in politics, not to mention for open military intervention in politics or military rule (see Shin and Park 2008, Shin and Wells 2005).

The only conceivable situation in which a serious civil-military crisis is likely to erupt in the foreseeable future would be a radical worsening of the security situation in Northeast Asia or a catastrophic handling of defense affairs by the civilian government. If the military leadership (and the general population) came to the conclusion that civilian leaders had compromised national security in the face of increasing tensions in inter-Korean or cross-strait relations, serious fallout could ensue for relations between the military and the elected rulers. This does not mean that the military would intervene in politics; such a scenario is highly unlikely. However, the military could attempt to recover its former decision-making powers and autonomy in defense and military policy in order to keep civilians out of these areas.

The further development of Indonesia is much less clear-cut. Despite the impressive progress made in the initial years after the transition and the early Yudhoyono years, civilian control still seems to depend on the president's ability to foster personal loyalty. Moreover, many organizational reforms have been bought with an increase in the military budget, a raise in military pay, acquiescence to continued military business activities, and reluctance to prosecute military personnel for crimes including human rights abuses.

Depending on the future development of Indonesian democracy, two scenarios seem possible. Should the political process, and especially Yudhoyono's succession in 2014, become more contentious, competitors could be tempted to use their personal connections to the military for political ends, akin to the current situation in the Philippines. Should Yudhoyono decide to push his reformist credentials or be succeeded by a democratic reformer, Indonesia could move along a path comparable to that of South Korea. While a soft approach could avoid an aggressive military reaction to the loss of its remaining privileges and might reduce civil-military conflict in the short run, a more robust approach will, in the long run, be the only way to eradicate the threat of military intervention and guarantee effective governance of security affairs.

Endnotes

1. This paper builds on the authors' previously published research (Croissant and Kuehn 2009; Croissant et al. 2010; Croissant, Kuehn, et al. 2011), but provides fresh theoretical insights, more recent data, and more in-depth analysis. Additional theoretical and conceptual discussions, empirical analyses, and intra- and inter-regional comparisons are provided in Croissant et al. (forthcoming). The research is part of a project sponsored by the German Research Fund (DFG, grant number CR 128/4-1). The authors would like to thank three reviewers for their helpful suggestions on an earlier draft of the manuscript and Paul Chambers and Siegfried Wolf, their colleagues in the DFG research project. A first draft was written and presented at the East-West Center, Honolulu, Hawai'i, where Aurel Croissant was a visiting fellow. Aurel is particularly grateful to Carolyn Eguchi and Denny Roy for their invaluable support during his stay and to the participants of the seminar in which this research was presented. He is especially indebted to the POSCO Foundation, which sponsored his fellowship. Philip Lorenz would like to thank Tanja Eschenauer for her assistance in compiling data on military representation in Indonesian politics.

2. The terms "armed forces" and "military" are used interchangeably in this study. "Military" refers to all permanent state organizations that are authorized by law to apply coercive power to defend the state against external threats, and their members. "Civilian" refers to all organizations of the state apparatus that are not attached to the military and that have the authority to formulate, implement, and oversee political decisions. This includes the legislative and executive branches, as well as the individual members of these institutions (Edmonds 1988). In the real world, this distinction is sometimes blurred. In Israel, for example, there is a prevalent practice known as "parachuting," in which former military leaders join the top echelons of political parties and cabinets (Etzioni-Halevy 1996: 406–413). In South Korea (1987) and Indonesia (2004), former military officers were elected president. However, as long as former military officers do not achieve office through military appointment, blackmail, or use of force, but are freely elected (usually as candidates of civilian political parties), they can be considered civilian politicians. The authors thank Hans Born for raising this issue.

3. The Economist Intelligence Unit's *Democracy Index 2010* ranks Taiwan as a flawed democracy. However, most quantitative democracy indices and many global and regional comparative studies classify Taiwan as a full-fledged liberal democracy (e.g., Gilley, Diamond and Chen 2008; Siaroff 2009; Freedom House 2011; Marshall and Cole 2011; Bertelsmann Stiftung 2012). This study shares the latter group's more positive evaluation of Taiwan's democracy.

4. Asia did not see any transitions to democracy in the "first long wave" that stretches from American independence or the early 19th century to the inter-war years (cf. Berg-Schlosser 2009).

5. In 1963, Park had ordered Chun to found an organization for Korean Military Academy graduates. Apart from his own classmates (class 11 of 1955) Chun also included the junior classes and named it the Hanahoe (Group One). Eligibility was limited to about 10 or 12 graduates from each class and restricted to those from Taegu and North Kyongsang Provinces, and required unanimous approval by existing members. In 1979, the group had about 240 members or 4.4 percent of the total number of Academy graduates since 1955, all from the graduating classes of 1955 to 1980 (I. Kim 2008: 59, 124).

6. Detailed accounts of how civil-military relations have developed since the transition from authoritarianism can be found in Croissant et al. (forthcoming).

7. Armed auxiliary groups fulfill major counterinsurgency roles in the Philippines. The Citizen Armed Force Geographical Units are under military command, while the Civilian Volunteer Organizations serve under the authority of the national police (Kraft 2010: 186–188).

8. For an overview, see Lambert 2009; Croissant, Kuehn, et al. 2011. Bruneau (2012) summarizes four essential criticisms: (1) the tautological nature of Huntington's argument about the relationship of professionalism and control; (2) the use of selective data and disparate factual evidence; (3) the failure of Huntington's approach to provide either empirically valid theoretical explanations or practical guidance for the reform of civil-military relations in democratic and democratizing countries; and (4) the "exclusive focus on civilian control of the armed forces" (ibid., 8). The current authors agree that civilian control is not the only problem of civil-military relations, but it is the most pressing one for new democracies, and without it all other civil-military challenges (such as efficiency and effectiveness) are irrelevant.

9. For additional discussion of the methodological and theoretical questions related to this debate and how the literature on civil-military relations literature has dealt with them, see Pion-Berlin (2001), Croissant and Kuehn (2011a) and Croissant et al. (forthcoming). For a general discussion of the structure and agency problem in social science, see Dessler (1989).

10. Confirmation of presidential appointments by the National Assembly was not required before March 2008. Since then, only the appointment of the chairman of the Joint Chiefs of Staff has required parliamentary approval (W. Kim 2008: 167).

Bibliography

Agüero, Felipe. 1995. *Soldiers, Civilians, and Democracy: Post-Franco Spain in Comparative Perspective*. Baltimore: Johns Hopkins University Press.

———. 1998. "Legacies of Transitions: Institutionalization, the Military, and Democracy in South America." *Mershon International Studies Review* 42(2): 383–404.

———. 2001. "Institutions, Transitions, and Bargaining: Civilians and the Military in Shaping Post-authoritarian Regimes." In Pion-Berlin, David, ed. 2001. *Civil-Military Relations in Latin America: New Analytical Perspectives*. Chapel Hill: University of North Carolina Press.

Alagappa, Muthiah. 2001a. "Introduction." In Alagappa, Muthiah, ed. 2001. *Coercion and Governance: The Declining Political Role of the Military in Asia*. Stanford: Stanford University Press.

———. 2001b. "Investigating and Explaining Change: An Analytical Framework." In Alagappa, Muthiah, ed. 2001. *Coercion and Governance: The Declining Political Role of the Military in Asia*. Stanford: Stanford University Press.

Anderson, Benedict. 1998. *The Specter of Comparison: Nationalism, Southeast Asia, and the World*. London: Verso.

Arugay, Aries. 2010. "Spheres of Military Autonomy under Democratic Rule: Implications and Prospects for Security Sector Transformation (SST) in the Philippines." *New Voices Series*, August 5.

———. 2011. "Saviors or Spoilers? Explaining 'Civil Society Coups' in an Age of Democratization." Paper presented at the First International Conference on International Relations and Development, Bangkok, May 19–20.

Aspinall, Edward. 2005. *Opposing Suharto: Compromise, Resistance, and Regime Change in Indonesia*. Stanford: Stanford University Press.

Aspinall, Edward, and Marcus Mietzner, eds. 2010. *Problems of Democratisation in Indonesia: Elections, Institutions and Society*. Singapore: Institute of Southeast Asian Studies.

Avudh, Panananda. 2006. "Thailand's Dept. Of Homeland Security," *The Nation*, December 12, http://www.nationmultimedia.com/politics/thailand-s-Dept-of-homeland-security-30021304.html.

Barany, Zoltan. 1997. "Democratic Consolidation and the Military: The Eastern European Experience." *Comparative Politics* 30(1): 31–43.

Barracca, Steven. 2007. "Military Coups in the Post–Cold War Era: Pakistan, Ecuador and Venezuela." *Third World Quarterly* 28(1): 137–54.

Bechtol, Bruce E. 2005. "Civil-Military Relations in the Republic of Korea." *Korea Observer* 36(4): 603–30.

Berg-Schlosser, Dirk. 2009. "Long Waves and Conjunctures of Democratization." In Haerpfer, Christian W., Patrick Bernhagen, Ronald F. Inglehart, and Christian Welzel, eds. 2009. *Democratization*. Oxford: Oxford University Press.

Berlin, Donald L. 2008. *Before Gringo: History of the Philippine Military, 1830–1972*. Manila: Anvil.

Bertelsmann Stiftung. 2012. *Bertelsmann Transformation Index (BTI), Country Reports, 2012*, http://www.bertelsmann-transformation-index.de/en/bti/country-reports/ /.

Betz, David. 2004. *Civil-Military Relations in Russia and Eastern Europe*. London: RoutledgeCurzon.

BICC (Bonn International Center for Conversion). 2006. *Security Sector Reform in Indonesia. Brief Country Studies*. Bonn: BICC, http://www.bicc.de/ssr_gtz/pdf/indonesia.pdf.

Bland, Douglas L. 1999. "A Unified Theory Of Civil-Military Relations." *Armed Forces & Society* 26(1): 7–25.

Braun, Sebastian. 2008. *Indonesia's Presidential Democracy*. Berlin: dissertation.de.

Bruneau, Thomas C. 2005. "Civil-Military Relations in Latin America: The Hedgehog and the Fox Revisited." *Revista Fuerzas Armadas y Sociedad* 19(1): 111–31.

———. 2012. "Impediments to the Accurate Conceptualization of Civil-Military Relations." In Bruneau, Thomas C., and Chris Matei, eds. *Handbook of Civil-Military Relations*. London: Routledge.

Bruneau, Thomas C., and Richard B. Goetze. 2006. "Civil-Military Relations in Latin America." *Military Review* (September–October): 67–74.

Bruneau, Thomas C., and Harold Trinkunas. 2006. "Democratization as a Global Phenomenon and Its Impact on Civil-Military Relations." *Democratization* 13(5): 776–90.

Bullard, Monte R. 1997. *The Soldier and the Citizen: The Role of the Military in Taiwan's Development*. Armonk: M.E. Sharpe.

Case, William. 2011. *Executive Accountability in Southeast Asia: The Role of Legislatures in New Democracies and Under Electoral Authoritarianism*. East-West-Center Policy Studies 57. Honolulu: East-West-Center.

Chai-anan, Samudavanija. 1982. *The Thai Young Turks.* Singapore: Institute of Southeast Asian Studies.

———. 1995. "Thailand: A Stable Semi-democracy." In Diamond, Larry, Juan J. Linz, and Seymour Martin Lipset, eds. 1995. *Politics in Developing Countries.* Boulder: Lynne Rienner.

Chambers, Paul W. 2010a. "Thailand on the Brink: Resurgent Military, Eroded Democracy." *Asian Survey* 50(5): 835–58.

———. 2010b. "U-Turn to the Past? The Resurgence of the Military in Contemporary Thai Politics." In Chambers, Paul W., and Aurel Croissant, eds. 2010. *Democracy under Stress: Civil-Military Relations in South and Southeast Asia.* Bangkok: ISIS.

Chase, Michael S. 2005. "Defense Reform in Taiwan: Problems and Prospects." *Asian Survey* 45(3): 362–82.

Chen, York W. 2010. "Civilian Control without a Civilian Defense Minister: A Narrative of the Interplays of Structure and Agency in Taiwan's Civil-Military Relations, 2000–2008." Paper prepared for the workshop Addressing the Structure-Agency Divide in the Study of Civil-Military Relations in Democratizing Asia, Heidelberg, October 14–15.

Ciron, Ruben F. 1993. "Civil-Military Relations in the Philippines." PhD dissertation, University of the Philippines.

Collier, Kit. 1999. *The Armed Forces and Internal Security in Asia: Preventing the Abuse of Power.* East-West Center Occasional Papers, Politics and Security Series, no. 2. Honolulu: East-West Center, http://scholarspace.manoa.hawaii.edu/ bitstream/10125/3451/ 1/PSop002.pdf.

Colton, Timothy J. 1979. *Commissars, Commanders, and Civilian Authority: The Structure of Soviet Military Politics.* Cambridge: Harvard University Press.

Croissant, Aurel. 2004. "Riding the Tiger: Civilian Control and the Military in Democratizing Korea." *Armed Forces & Society* 30(3): 357–81.

———. 2007. "Muslim Insurgency, Political Violence, and Democracy in Thailand." *Terrorism and Political Violence* 19(1): 1–18.

———. 2008. "Soziale Gruppen, Politische Kraefte und die Demokratie. Eine Strukturorientierte Analyse Demokratischer Transformation in Thailand." *Journal of Contemporary Southeast Asia* 1: 3–37.

———. 2011. "Types of Democracy in Southeast Asia and Democratic Consolidation." In Croissant, Aurel, and Marco Bünte, eds. 2011. *The Crisis of Democratic Governance in Southeast Asia.* Houndsmills, Basingstoke, Hampshire: Palgrave Macmillan.

Croissant, Aurel and Marco Bünte 2011. "Introduction." In Croissant, Aurel, and Marco Bünte, eds. 2011. *The Crisis of Democratic Governance in Southeast Asia.* Houndsmills, Basingstoke, Hampshire: Palgrave Macmillan.

Croissant, Aurel, and Marco Bünte, eds. 2011. *The Crisis of Democratic Governance in Southeast Asia.* Houndsmills, Basingstoke, Hampshire: Palgrave Macmillan.

Croissant, Aurel, and David Kuehn. 2009. "Patterns of Civilian Control in East Asia's New Democracies." *Journal of East Asian Studies* 9(2): 187–217.

Croissant, Aurel, and David Kuehn. 2011a. "Guest Editors' Introduction: Civil-Military Relations in Democratizing Asia—Structure, Agency and the Struggle for Civilian Control." *Asian Journal of Political Science Special Issue*, 19(3): 213–21.

———. 2011b. *Militär und Zivile Politik* [The military and civilian politics]. Munich: Oldenbourg.

Croissant, Aurel, David Kuehn, Paul W. Chambers, Philip Völkel, and Siegfried O. Wolf. 2011. "Theorizing Civilian Control of the Military in Emerging Democracies: Agency, Structure and Institutional Change." *Zeitschrift für Vergleichende Politikwissenschaft* 5(1): 75–98.

Croissant, Aurel, David Kuehn, Paul Chambers, and Siegfried O. Wolf. 2010. "Beyond the Fallacy of Coup-ism: Conceptualizing Civilian Control of the Military in Emerging Democracies." *Democratization* 17(5), 948–78.

Croissant, Aurel, David Kuehn, Philip Lorenz, and Paul W. Chambers. forthcoming. *Struggling for Civilian Control in Democratizing Asia*. Basingstoke: Palgrave.

Croissant, Aurel, and Philip Völkel. 2012. "Party System Types and Party System Institutionalization: Comparing New Democracies in East and Southeast Asia." *Party Politics* 18(2), 235–65.

Croissant, Aurel, Philip Völkel, and Paul Chambers 2011. "Democracy, the Military, and Security Sector Governance in Indonesia, the Philippines, and Thailand." In Croissant, Aurel, and Marco Bünte, eds. 2011. *The Crisis of Democratic Governance in Southeast Asia*. Houndsmills, Basingstoke, Hampshire: Palgrave Macmillan.

Crouch, Harold. 1979. "Patrimonialism and Military Rule in Indonesia." *World Politics* 31(4): 571–87.

Dahl, Robert A. 1971. *Polyarchy: Participation and Opposition*. New Haven: Yale University Press.

De Castro, Renato Cruz. 2005. "The Dilemma between Democratic Control versus Military Reforms: The Case of the AFP Modernization Program, 1991–2004." *Journal of Security Sector Management* 3(1): 1–24.

———. 2010. "The Context of 21st Century Philippine Civil-Military Relations: Why Partnership Instead of Subordination?" Paper presented at the workshop *Addressing the Structure-Agency Divide in the Study of Civil-Military Relations in Democratizing Asia*, Institute of Political Science and the South Asia Institute of Ruprecht-Karls-University, Heidelberg, October 14–15.

Desch, Michael C. 1999. *Civilian Control of the Military: The Changing Security Environment*. Baltimore: Johns Hopkins University Press.

Dessler, David. 1989. "What's at Stake in the Agent-Structure Debate?" *International Organisation* 43(3): 441–73.

Dharmono, B. 2010. Personal interview with Lt. Gen. (ret.) Bambang Dharmono, former commander of military operations in Aceh and former secretary general of National Defense Council, September 15, Bogor, Indonesia.

Diamond, Larry. 2002. "Thinking about Hybrid Regimes." *Journal of Democracy* 13(2): 21–35.

———. 2008. *The Spirit of Democracy: The Struggle to Build Free Societies Throughout the World.* New York: Henry Holt.

Economist Intelligence Unit. 2010. *Democracy Index 2010: Democracy in Retreat,* http://graphics.eiu.com/PDF/Democracy_Index_2010_web.pdf.

Editors. 2008. "Current Data on the Indonesian Military Elite, September 2005–March 2008." *Indonesia* 85 (April): 79–121.

Edmonds, Martin. 1988. *Armed Services and Society.* Leicester: Leicester University.

Etzioni-Halevy, Eva. 1996. "Civil-Military Relations and Democracy: The Case of the Military-Political Elites' Connection in Israel." *Armed Forces & Society* 22(3): 401–417.

Ezrow, Natasha M., and Erica Franz. 2011. *Dictators and Dictatorships. Understanding Authoritarian Regimes and Their Leaders.* New York: Continuum.

Feaver, Peter. 1996. "The Civil-Military Problematique: Huntington, Janowitz, and the Question of Civilian Control." *Armed Forces & Society* 23(2): 149–78.

———. 1999. "Civil-Military Relations." *Annual Review of Political Science* 2(1): 211–41.

———. 2003. *Armed Servants: Agency, Oversight, and Civil-Military Relations.* Cambridge: Harvard University Press.

Finer, Samuel E. 1962. *The Man on Horseback: The Role of the Military in Politics.* Boulder: Westview Press.

Fitch, Samuel J. 1998. *The Armed Forces and Democracy in Latin America.* Baltimore: Johns Hopkins University Press.

Forster, Anthony. 2006. *Armed Forces and Society in Europe.* Basingstoke: Palgrave.

Fravel, M. Taylor. 2002. "Towards Civilian Supremacy: Civil-Military Relations in Taiwan's Democratization." *Armed Forces & Society* 29(1): 57–84.

Freedom House. 2011. *Freedom in the World 2011. The Annual Survey of Political Rights and Civil Liberties.* Lanham: Rowman & Littlefield.

Geddes, Barbara. 1999. "What Do We Know About Democratization after Twenty Years?" *Annual Review of Political Science* 2(1): 115–44.

Gilley, Bruce, Larry J. Diamond, and Weitseng Chen, eds. 2008. *Political Change in China: Comparisons with Taiwan.* Stanford: Stanford University Press.

Gloria, Glenda. 1999. *The RAM Boys: Where Are They Now?* Quezon City: Philippine Center for Investigative Journalism, http://pcij.org/stories/1999/ram.html.

———. 2003. *We Were Soldiers: Military Men in Politics and the Bureaucracy.* Quezon City: Friedrich Ebert Foundation.

Graham, Norman A. 1991. "The Role of the Military in the Political and Economic Development of the Republic of Korea." *Journal of Asian and African Studies* 26(1–2): 114–31.

Hadenius, Axel and Jan Teorell. 2006. "Authoritarian Regimes: Stability, Change, and Pathways to Democracy, 1972-2003." Kellogg Institute Working Paper (331).

Hadi, Bambang. 2010. Personal interview with Bambang Hadi, professor, Indonesian Defense University, September 1, Jakarta, Indonesia.

Hadiz, Vedi R. 2010. *Localising Power in Post-authoritarian Indonesia: A Southeast Asia Perspective*. Stanford: Stanford University Press.

Hall, Rosalie A. 2010. "Boots on Unstable Ground: Democratic Governance of Armed Forces under Post-9/11 US-Philippines Military Relations." *Asia-Pacific Social Sciences Review* 10(2): 25–42.

Han, Sung-joo. 1974. *The Failure of Democracy in South Korea*. Berkeley: University of California Press.

Hänggi, Heiner. 2004. "Conceptualising Security Sector Reform and Reconstruction." In Bryden, Alan, and Heiner Hänggi, eds. 2004. *Reform and Reconstruction of the Security Sector*. Münster: LIT Verlag.

Hay, Colin. 2002. *Political Analysis: A Critical Introduction*. Basingstoke: Palgrave.

Hay, Colin, and Daniel Wincott. 1998. "Structure, Agency and Historical Institutionalism." *Political Studies* 46: 951–57.

Hedman, Eva-Lotta. 2001. "The Philippines: Not So Military, Not So Civil." In Alagappa, Muthiah, ed. 2001. *Coercion and Governance: The Declining Political Role of the Military in Asia*. Stanford: Stanford University Press.

Henry, Clement M., and Robert Springborg. 2001. *Globalization and Politics of Development in the Middle East*. Cambridge: Cambridge University Press.

Hernandez, Carolina G. 2002. "Restoring Democratic Civilian Control over the Philippine Military: Challenges and Prospects." *Journal of International Cooperation Studies* 10(1): 25–48.

———. 2005. "Security Sector Governance and Practices in Asia." *Journal of Security Sector Management* 3(1), http://www.ssronline.org/jofssm/issues/jofssm_sp_03_asia_hernandez.pdf.

———. 2007. "The Military in Philippine Politics: Retrospect and Prospects." In Salazar, Lorraine Carlos, and Rodolfo C. Severino, eds. 2007. *Whither the Philippines in the 21st Century*. Singapore: Institute for Southeast Asian Studies.

Hernandez, Katherine Marie G., and Herman Joseph S. Kraft. 2010. "Armed Forces as Veto Power: Civil-Military Relations in the Philippines." In Chambers, Paul W., and Aurel Croissant, eds. 2010. *Democracy under Stress: Civil-Military Relations in South and Southeast Asia*. Bangkok: ISIS.

Hicken, Allen, and Erik Martinez Kuhonta. 2011. "Shadows from the Past: Party System Institutionalization in Asia." *Comparative Political Studies* 44(5): 572–97.

Honna, Jun. 2003. *Military Politics and Democratization in Indonesia.* RoutledgeCurzon Research on Southeast Asia 4. London: RoutledgeCurzon.

————. 2006. "Local Civil-Military Relations during the First Phase of Democratic Transition, 1999–2004: A Comparison of West, Central, and East Java." *Indonesia* 82(October): 75–96.

Hsueh, Chao-yung. 2003. "National Identity and Conflicting Loyalty and Obedience in the ROC Armed Forces." *Issues and Studies* 39(4): 145–62.

Human Rights Watch. 2006. *Too High a Price: The Human Rights Cost of the Indonesian Military's Economic Activities.* New York: Human Rights Watch.

Hung, Lu-hsun, Ta-hua Mo, and Fu-chu Tuan. 2003. "The Evolution of the ROC's Military Societal Relations: From Militarized Society to Socialized Military." In Edmonds, Michael, and Michael M. Tsai, eds. 2003. *Defending Taiwan: The Future of Taiwan's Defense Policy and Military Strategy.* New York: Routledge.

Hunter, Wendy. 1997. *Eroding Military Influence in Brazil: Politicians Against Soldiers.* Chapel Hill: University of North Carolina Press.

Huntington, Samuel P. 1957. *The Soldier and the State: The Theory and Politics of Civil-Military Relations.* Cambridge: Belknap Press of Harvard University Press.

————. 1991. *The Third Wave: Democratization in the Late Twentieth Century.* Norman: University of Oklahoma Press.

Hutchcroft, Paul D. 2000. *Booty Capitalism: The Politics of Banking in the Philippines.* Manila: Ateneo de Manila University Press.

————. 2008. "The Arroyo Imbroglio in the Philippines." *Journal of Democracy*, 19(1): 141–55.

Jakarta Post. 1999. *A Who's Who of Members of the National Unity Cabinet,* October 27, http://www.thejakartapost.com/news/1999/10/27/a-who039s-who-members-national-unity-cabinet.html.

————. 2000. *Brief Profile of Gus Dur's Reshuffled Cabinet,* August 24, http://www.thejakartapost.com/news/2000/08/24/brief-profile-gus-dur039s-reshuffled-cabinet.html.

————. 2001a. *Gus Dur Names Lopa as New Justice Minister,* February 9, http://www.thejakartapost.com/news/2001/02/09/gus-dur-names-lopa-new-justice-minister.html.

————. 2001b. *Susilo Replaced in Hasty Reshuffle,* June 2, http://www.thejakartapost.com/news/2001/06/02/susilo-replaced-hasty-reshuffle.html.

————. 2004. *The United Indonesia Cabinet 2004–2009,* October 22, http://www.thejakartapost.com/news/2004/10/22/united-indonesia-cabinet-20042009.html.

————. 2009. *United Indonesia Cabinet 2009–2014,* October 22, http://www.thejakartapost.com/news/2009/10/22/united-indonesia-cabinet-20092014.html.

Jansen, David. 2008. "Relations among Security and Law Enforcement Institutions in Indonesia." *Contemporary Southeast Asia* 30(3): 429–54.

Joo, Rudolf. 1995. "The Democratic Control of Armed Forces." Chaillot Paper 23: Institute for Security Studies, Western European Union.

Jun, Jinsok. 2001. "Korea: Consolidating Democratic Civilian Control." In Alagappa, Muthiah, ed. 2001. *Coercion and Governance: The Declining Political Role of the Military in Asia.* Stanford: Stanford University Press.

Kamvara, Mehran. 2000. "Military Professionalization and Civil-Military Relations in the Middle East." *Political Science Quarterly* 115(1): 67–92.

Kepres. 1998. Keputusan Presiden Republik Indonesia Nomor 62/M Tahun 1998.

———. 1999. Keputusan Presiden Republik Indonesia Nomor 355/M Tahun 1999.

———. 2000. Keputusan Presiden Republik Indonesia Nomor 234/M Tahun 2000.

———. 2004. Keputusan Presiden Republik Indonesia Nomor 187/M Tahun 2004.

———. 2007. Keputusan Presiden Republik Indonesia Nomor 31/P Tahun 2007.

———. 2009. Keputusan Presiden Republik Indonesia Nomor 84/P Tahun 2009.

Kim, Insoo. 2008. *Bringing the Military Back in Political Transition: Democratic Transition by and for Powerless Officers in South Korea.* PhD dissertation, University of Wisconsin-Madison.

Kim, Kijoo. 2009. *Post–Cold War Civil-Military Relations in South Korea: Toward a Postmodern Military?* PhD dissertation, State University of New York at Buffalo.

Kim, Wooksung. 2008. "The Conditions for Successful Civilian Control over the Military in New Democracies: The Case of South Korea." *Quarterly Journal of Defense Policy Studies* 24(4): 151–75.

Kim, Yong Cheol, R. William Liddle, and Salim Said. 2006. "Political Leadership and Civilian Supremacy in Third Wave Democracies: Comparing South Korea and Indonesia." *Pacific Affairs* 79: 247–68.

Kim, Young Min. 2004. "Patterns of Military Rule and Prospects for Democracy in South Korea." In May, Ronald James, and Viberti Selochan, eds. 2004. *The Military and Democracy in Asia and the Pacific.* Canberra: ANU E Press.

Kingsbury, Damien. 2003. *Power Politics and the Indonesian Military.* London: Routledge.

Kohn, Richard H. 1997. "How Democracies Control the Military." *Journal of Democracy* 8(4): 140–53.

Kraft, J. Hermann S. 2010. "The Foibles of an Armed Citizenry: Armed Auxiliaries of the State and Private Armed Groups in the Philippines (Overview)." In Santos, Soliman M., and Paz Verdades Santos, eds. 2010. *Primed and Purposeful: Armed Groups and Human Security in the Philippines.* Geneva: Small Arms Survey.

Kuehn, David. 2008. "Democratization and Civilian Control of the Military in Taiwan." *Democratization* 15(5): 870–90.

Kuehn, David, and Philip Lorenz. 2011. "Explaining Civil-Military Relations in New Democracies: Structure, Agency and Theory Development." *Asian Journal of Social Science* 19(3): 231–49.

Lambert, Alexandre. 2009. *Democratic Civilian Control of Armed Forces in the Post-Cold War Era*. Vienna: LIT.

Landé, Carl H. 2001. "The Return of 'People Power' in the Philippines." *Journal of Democracy* 12(2): 88–102.

Lee, Mannwoo. 1990. *The Odyssey of Korean Democracy: Korean Politics, 1987–1990*. New York: Praeger.

Lee, Terence. 2009. "Armed Forces and Transitions from Authoritarian Rule: Explaining the Role of the Military in 1986 Philippines and 1998 Indonesia." *Comparative Political Studies* 42(5): 640–69.

Lee, Wei-chin. 2007. "The Greening of the Brass: Taiwan's Civil-Military Relations since 2000." *Asian Security* 3(3): 204–227.

Levitsky, Steven, and Lucan A. Way. 2010. *Competitive Authoritarianism: Hybrid Regimes after the Cold War*. Cambridge: Cambridge University Press.

Lihkit, Dhiravegin. 1992. *Demi-Democracy: The Evolution of the Thai Political System. Thai Politics in Transition*. Singapore: Time Academic Press.

Lo, Chih-cheng. 2001. "Taiwan: The Remaining Challenges." In Alagappa, Muthiah, ed. 2001. *Coercion and Governance: The Declining Political Role of the Military in Asia*. Stanford: Stanford University Press.

Loveman, Brian. 1999. *For La Patria: Politics and the Armed Forces in Latin America*. Wilmington, DE: Scholarly Resources.

Mahroza, Jonni. 2009. *A Local Perspective on Military Withdrawal from Politics in Indonesia: East Java 1998–2003*. Saarbrücken: Lambert Academic Publishing.

Makaarim, Mufti A., and S. Yunanto, eds. 2008. *The Effectiveness of Civil Society Organization Advocacy Strategies in Security Sector Reform in Indonesia 1998–2006*. Jakarta: Institute for Defence Security and Peace Studies.

Mares, David R. 1998. "Civil-Military Relations, Democracy, and the Regional Neighborhood." In Mares, David R., ed. 1998. *Civil-Military Relations: Building Democracy and Regional Security in Latin America, Southern Asia, and Central Europe*. Boulder: Westview Press.

Marshall, Monty G., and Benjamin R. Cole. 2011. *Global Report 2011: Conflict, Governance and State Fragility*. Vienna: Center for Systemic Peace, http://www.systemicpeace.org/GlobalReport2011.pdf.

McCargo, Duncan, and Pathmanand Ukrist. 2005. *The Thaksinization of Thailand: Studies in Contemporary Asian History*. Copenhagen: NIAS Press.

McCoy, Alfred. 2000. *Closer than Brothers: Manhood at the Philippine Military Academy*. New Haven: Yale University Press.

McGregor, Katharine E. 2007. *History in Uniform: Military Ideology and the Construction of Indonesia's Past*. Honolulu: University of Hawaii Press.

McLeod, Ross H. 2008. "Inadequate Budgets and Salaries as Instruments for Institutionalizing Public Sector Corruption in Indonesia." *South East Asia Research* 16(2): 199–223.

Merkel, Wolfgang. 2004. "Embedded and Defective Democracies." *Democratization* 11(5): 33–58.

Mietzner, Marcus. 2009. *Military Politics, Islam and the State in Indonesia: From Turbulent Transition to Democratic Consolidation*. Leiden: KITLV Press.

———. 2011. "Overcoming Path Dependence. The Quality of Civilian Control of the Military in Post-Authoritarian Indonesia." *Asian Journal of Political Science* 19 (3):270–89.

Miller, Michelle Ann. 2009. *Rebellion and Reform in Indonesia: Jakarta's Security and Autonomy Policies in Aceh*. London: Routledge.

Miranda, Felipe B. 1992. *The Politicization of the Military*. Social Weather Station Occasional Papers. Quezon City: Social Weather Station.

Moon, Chung-In, and Kang, Mun-gu. 1995. "Democratic Opening and Military Intervention in South Korea: Comparative Assessment and Implications." In Cotton, James, ed. 1995. *Politics and Policy in the New Korean State: From Roh Tae-Woo to Kim Young-Sam*. New York: St. Martin's Press.

Moon, Chung-In, and Sang-young Rhyu. 2011. "Democratic Transition, Persistent Civilian Control over the Military, and the South Korean Anomaly." *Asian Journal of Political Science* 19 (3):250–69.

Murray, David. 1996. *Angels and Devils: Thai Politics from February 1991 to September 1992, A Struggle for Democracy?* Bangkok: White Orchid Press.

Nordlinger, Eric A. 1977. *Soldiers in Politics: Military Coups and Governments*. Englewood Cliffs: Prentice Hall.

Ockey, James. 2001. "Thailand: The Struggle to Redefine Civil-Military Relations." In Alagappa, Muthiah, ed. 2001. *Coercion and Governance: The Declining Political Role of the Military in Asia*. Stanford: Stanford University Press.

Ooi, Sue Mae 2010. "The Transnational Protection Regime and Democratic Breakthrough: A Comparative Study of Taiwan, South Korea and Singapore." Thesis, University of Toronto.

Padgett, John, and Christopher Ansell. 1993. "Robust Action and the Rise of the Medici, 1400–1434." *American Journal of Sociology* 98: 1259–1319.

Pasuk, Phongpaichit, and Chris Baker. 2009. *Thaksin*, 2nd ed. Chiang Mai: Silkworm Books.

PCIJ (Philippine Center for Investigative Journalism). 2011. *Out of the Barracks and into the Pits*. The PCIJ Series on Military Corruption 25 Years after People Power, http://pcij.org/stories/on-edsas-25th-corruption-devours-the-armed-forces/.

Perlmutter, Amos, and William M. LeoGrande. 1982. "The Party in Uniform: Toward a Theory of Civil-Military Relations in Communist Political Systems." *American Political Science Review* 76(4): 778–89.

Pion-Berlin, David. 1997. *Through the Corridors of Power: Institutions and Civil-Military Relations in Argentina*. University Park: Pennsylvania State University Press.

———, ed. 2001. *Civil-Military Relations in Latin America: New Analytical Perspectives*. Chapel Hill: University of North Carolina Press.

———. 2003. "A New Civil-Military Pragmatism in Latin America." Unpublished manuscript on file with author.

———. 2005. "Political Management of the Military in Latin America." *Military Review* (January–February): 19–31.

———. 2011. "The Study of Civil-Military Relations in New Democracies." *Asian Journal of Political Science* 19(3): 222–30.

Pion-Berlin, David, and Harold Trinkunas. 2007. "Attention Deficits: Why Politicians Ignore Defense Policy in Latin America." *Latin American Research Review* 42(3): 76–100.

Pohlman, Annie. 2010. *Indonesia and Post–New Order Reforms: Challenges and Opportunities for Promoting the Responsibility to Protect*. Research Report on Indonesia 1, Asia-Pacific Center for the Responsibility to Protect, http://www.r2pasiapacific.org/documents/Indonesia%20Report%20No%20 1%20July%202010%20FINAL.pdf.

Powell, Jonathan M., and Clayton L. Thyne. 2011. "Global Instances of Coups from 1950 to 2010: A New Dataset." *Journal of Peace Research* 48(2): 249–59.

Rabasa, Angel M., and John B. Haseman. 2002. *The Military and Democracy in Indonesia: Challenges, Politics, and Power*. Santa Monica: RAND.

Raska, Michael. 2011. "RMA Diffusion Paths and Patterns in South Korea's Military Modernization." *Korean Journal of Defense Analysis* 23(3): 369–85.

Rasmussen, Maria J. 1999. *The Military Role in Internal Defense and Security: Some Problems*. CCMR Occasional Paper 6. Monterey: Naval Postgraduate School.

Robles, Alan C. 2008. "The Elephant in the Living Room." *Development and Cooperation* 49(10): 371–73.

Said, Salim. 2006. *Legitimizing Military Rule: Indonesian Armed Forces Ideology, 1958–2000*. Jakarta: Pustaka Sinar Harapan.

Santos, Paz Verdades M. 2010. "The Communist Front: Protracted People's War and Counter-insurgency in the Philippines." In Santos, Soliman M., Jr., and Paz Verdades M. Santos, eds. 2010. *Primed and Purposeful: Armed Groups and Human Security Efforts in the Philippines*. Geneva: Small Arms Survey.

Saxer, Carl J. 2004. "Generals and Presidents: Establishing Civilian and Democratic Control in South Korea." *Armed Forces & Society* 30(3): 383–408.

Scarpello, Fabio. 2005. Thaksin's Power Play with Thai Generals. *Asia Times*, April 7. http://www.atimes.com/atimes/Southeast_Asia/GD07Ae01.html.

Schedler, Andreas. 2006. "The Logic of Electoral Authoritarianism." In Schedler, Andreas, ed. 2006. *Electoral Authoritarianism: The Dynamics of Unfree Competition*. Boulder: Lynne Rienner.

Sebastian, Leonard C., and Iisingdarsah. 2011. "Demilitarizing the State in Indonesia: Losing the Impetus for Reform?" Unpublished manuscript on file with the author.

Selochan, Viberto. 1998. "The Military and the Fragile Democracy of the Philippines." In May, Ronald J., and Viberto Selochan, eds. 1998. *The Military and Democracy in Asia and the Pacific*. Bathurst: Crawford House Publishing.

Shambaugh, David. 1996. "Taiwan's Security: Maintaining Deterrence amid Political Accountability." *The China Quarterly* 148: 1284–1318.

Sheingate, Adam D. 2007. "The Terrain of the Political Entrepreneur." In Skowronek, Stephen, and Matthew Glassman, eds. 2007. *Formative Acts: American Politics in the Making*. Philadelphia: University of Pennsylvania Press.

Shih, Cheng-Hsiao. 1990. *Party-Military Relations in the PRC and Taiwan: Paradoxes of Control*. Boulder: Westview Press.

Shin, Doh Chull and Chong-min Park. 2008. "The Mass Public and Democratic Politics in South Korea. Exploring the Subjective World of Democratization in Flux." In Chu, Yun-han, Larry J. Diamond, Andrew J. Nathan, and Doh Chull Shin, eds. 2008. *How East Asians View Democracy*. New York: Columbia University Press.

Shin, Doh Chull, and Rollin F. Tusalem. 2009. "Democratization in East Asia." In Haerpfer, Christian W., Patrick Bernhagen, Ronald F. Inglehart, and Christian Welzel, eds. 2009. *Democratization*. Oxford: Oxford University Press

Shin, Doh Chull, and Jason Wells. 2005. "Is Democracy the Only Game in Town?" *Journal of Democracy* 16 (2): 89–101.

Siaroff, Alan. 2009. *Comparing Political Regimes: A Thematic Introduction to Comparative Politics*, 2nd. ed. Toronto: University of Toronto Press.

Slater, Dan. 2010. "Altering Authoritarianism: Institutional Complexity and Autocratic Agency in Indonesia." In Mahoney, James, and Kathleen Thelen, eds. 2010. *Explaining Institutional Change: Ambiguity, Agency, and Power*. Cambridge: Cambridge University Press.

Stepan, Alfred. 1988. *Rethinking Military Politics: Brazil and the Southern Cone*. Princeton: Princeton University Press.

Surachart, Bamrungsuk. 1999. "From Dominance to Power Sharing: The Military and Politics in Thailand, 1973–1992." PhD thesis, Columbia University.

———. 2001. "Thailand: Military Professionalism at the Crossroads." In Alagappa, Muthiah, ed. 2001. *Military Professionalism in Asia: Conceptual and Empirical Perspectives*. Honolulu: East West Center.

Svolik, Milan W. 2009. "Power Sharing and Leadership Dynamics in Authoritarian Regimes." *American Journal of Political Science* 53(2):477–94.

Swaine, Michael D. 1999. *Taiwan's National Security, Defense Policy, and Weapons Procurement Processes*. RAND Monograph Reports. Santa Monica: RAND.

Swaine, Michael D., and James C. Mulvenon. 2001. *Taiwan's Foreign and Defense Policies : Features and Determinants*. Santa Monica: RAND.

Teodosio, Emmanuel R. 1997. "The AFP Rapid Maneuver Force: A Proposal towards Modernization." *National Security Review* 18(1): 28–79.

Thitinan, Pongsudhirak. 2008. "Thailand Since the Coup." *Journal of Democracy* 19(4): 140–53.

Thompson, Mark R. 1995. *The Anti-Marcos Struggle: Personalistic Rule and Democratic Transition in the Philippines.* New Haven: Yale University Press.

———. 2011. "Moore Meets Gramsci and Burke in Southeast Asia: New Democracies and Civil Society." In Croissant, Aurel, and Marco Bünte, eds. 2011. *The Crisis of Democratic Governance in Southeast Asia.* Basingstoke: Palgrave.

Tien, Hung-mao. 1989. *The Great Transition: Political and Social Change in the Republic of China.* Stanford: Hoover Institution Press, Stanford University.

Tiglao, Rigoberto. 1990. *Kudeta: The Challenge to Philippine Democracy.* Quezon City: Philippine Center for Investigative Journalism.

Tomsa, Dirk. 2008. *Party Politics and Democratization in Indonesia: Golkar in the Post-Suharto Era.* Routledge Contemporary Southeast Asia Series, no. 21. London: Routledge.

Tordecilla, Jaemark. 2011. *Sidebar: A Politicized Military.* Philippine Center for Investigative Journalism, http://pcij.org/stories/a-politicized-military/.

Traimas, Chaowana, and Jochen Hoerth. 2008. "Thailand: Another New Constitution as a Way Out of the Vicious Cycle?" In Hill, Clausopeter, and Jörg Menzel, eds. *Constitutionalism in Southeast Asia 2: Reports on National Constitutions.* Singapore: Konrad-Adenauer-Stiftung.

Trinkunas, Harold 2005. *Crafting Civilian Control of the Military in Venezuela: A Comparative Perspective.* Chapel Hill: University of North Carolina Press.

Tzeng, Yisuo. 2009. "Civil-Military Relations in Democratizing Taiwan, 1986–2007." PhD dissertation, George Washington University.

Ukrist, Pathmanand. 2008. "A Different Coup d'Etat?" *Journal of Contemporary Asia* 38(1): 124–42.

Valenzuela, Samuel J. 1992. "Democratic Consolidation in Post-Transitional Settings, Notion, Process, and Facilitating Conditions." In Mainwaring, Scott, and Guillermo A. O'Donnell, eds. 1992. *Issues in Democratic Consolidation: The New South American Democracies in Comparative Perspective.* Notre Dame: University of Notre Dame Press.

Wandelt, Ingo. 2007. "Security Sector Reform in Indonesia: Military vs. Civil Supremacy." In Hadiwinata, Bob S., and Christoph Schuck, eds. 2007. *Democracy in Indonesia: The Challenge of Consolidation.* Baden-Baden: Nomos.

Watts, Larry L. 2002. "Reforming Civil-Military Relations in Post-Communist States: Civil Control vs. Democratic Control." *Journal of Political and Military Sociology* 30(1): 51–70.

Wilkinson, Paul. 2006. *Terrorism Versus Democracy: The Liberal State Response,* 2nd. ed. London: Routledge.

Witular, Rendy A. 2011. Marciano Norman: Ending the Code of Silence at Spy Agency. *Jakarta Post*, December 22, http://www.thejakartapost.com/news/2011/12/22/marciano-norman-ending-code-silence-spy-agency.html.

Wu, Naiteh. 2005. "Transition without Justice, or Justice without History: Transitional Justice in Taiwan." *Taiwan Journal of Democracy* 1(1): 77–102.

Wyatt, David K. 1984. *A Short History of Thailand*, New Haven: Yale University Press.

Yawnghwe, Chao-Tzang. 1997. "The Politics of Authoritarianism: The State and Political Soldiers in Burma, Indonesia, and Thailand." PhD dissertation, University of British Columbia.

Policy Studies

an East-West Center series

Series Editors: *Edward Aspinall and Dieter Ernst*

Description

Policy Studies presents scholarly analysis of key contemporary domestic and international political, economic, and strategic issues affecting Asia in a policy relevant manner. Written for the policy community, academics, journalists, and the informed public, the peer-reviewed publications in this series provide new policy insights and perspectives based on extensive fieldwork and rigorous scholarship.

The East-West Center is pleased to announce that the Policy Studies series has been accepted for indexing in Web of Science Book Citation Index. The Web of Science is the largest and most comprehensive citation index available. The quality and depth of content Web of Science offers to researchers, authors, publishers, and institutions sets it apart from other research databases. The inclusion of Policy Studies in the Book Citation Index demonstrates our dedication to providing the most relevant and influential content to our community.

Notes to Contributors

Submissions may take the form of a proposal or complete manuscript. For more information on the Policy Studies series, please contact the Series Editors.

Editors, *Policy Studies*
East-West Center
1601 East-West Road
Honolulu, Hawai'i 96848-1601
Tel: 808.944.7197
Publications@EastWestCenter.org
EastWestCenter.org/PolicyStudies

www.ingramcontent.com/pod-product-compliance
Lightning Source LLC
Chambersburg PA
CBHW050559280326
41933CB00011B/1904